Review of Scottish Culture

Review of Scottish Culture

Edited by
ALEXANDER FENTON
with
Hugh Cheape and Rosalind K Marshall

Founded 1984 with the aid of a grant from the Allan Fund

JOHN DONALD PUBLISHERS LTD
and
NATIONAL MUSEUM OF ANTIQUITIES OF SCOTLAND
EDINBURGH

Address for Reviews, Correspondence, etc:
Editors, ROSC, National Museum of Antiquities of Scotland,
Queen Street, Edinburgh EH2 1JD

Address for Subscriptions:
John Donald Publishers Ltd, 138 St Stephen Street,
Edinburgh, EH3 5AA, Scotland

ROSC is published annually. It is a well-illustrated journal.
Price £5 per issue

Printed and bound in Great Britain by
Bell & Bain Ltd, Glasgow.

Editorial

The Review of Scottish Culture (ROSC) is a new journal that fills a real gap in the study of material culture. Scotland has a long history, covering ten thousand years. In the course of that time it has been greatly affected by the cultures of neighbouring peoples, some of them invaders. Scottish influence on the world at large, spread by the wandering Scot, has been proverbial. The Journal will, in its varied contributions, throw fresh light on these inward and outward movements, where necessary tracing them beyond the bounds of Scotland itself.

The acronym ROSC is appropriate, since its meaning in Gaelic relates to the action of seeing – vision, perception, understanding – and also to what is seen – the written word in prose. The essence of this philosophical sense will, we hope, be reflected in the Journal's contents.

ROSC concentrates on the material aspects of the country's social and economic history; the word widely used in Europe for these studies is 'ethnology'. The Journal covers rural and urban, maritime and land-based topics alike, the applied and decorative arts, graphics and design, and the actions and interactions of all sorts and conditions of men and women.

Attention is drawn to relevant books from home and abroad, in reviews and notes, to broaden existing historical perspectives. The contributions deal with original source material in a readable form, so that they can be read, used and enjoyed by specialists and all other readers.

The Editors

Contributors

R C Boud Geological Cartographer, Department of Earth Sciences, University of Leeds

Dr D J Breeze Inspector of Ancient Monuments, Scottish Development Department (Ancient Monuments Division)

R H Buchanan Department of Geography, Queen's University, Belfast

Dr R G Cant formerly Department of Scottish History, University of St Andrews

D Macdonald retired Headmaster, and a Lewis man

Dr A Fenton National Museum of Antiquities of Scotland

T Henderson formerly Curator, Shetland Museum, Lerwick

C Hendry Country Life Section, National Museum of Antiquities of Scotland

Rosalind K Marshall Scottish National Portrait Gallery

A Sharp Temporary Assistant, National Museum of Antiquities of Scotland

Contents

To Tom Henderson: A Fine Shetlander

The first issue of our Review of Scottish Culture is dedicated to the late Thomas Henderson, MBE, JP, FSA Scot, who died on 15th October, 1982. His loss is a loss to Scotland as well as to Shetland, for he was a man of many parts. He was born in 1911, went to school at Boddam, and then helped his parents for a few years before going to sea at the age of 19. After marrying Catherine (Katie) Mowat in 1938, he stayed ashore for a year, but returned to the sea when war broke out in the following year. As a result of being torpedoed, he was paralysed from the waist down for 3½ years.

He lost neither heart nor energy, but read everything he could lay hands on, and took to writing articles and stories in beautifully polished and highly readable prose, in journals such as *Chambers Journal*, *Argosy* and *Sea Breeze*.

He returned to full health, and for a time he and Katie ran the hotel that had been his parents', at Spiggie, where visitors returned again and again to enjoy the hospitality and to take the benefit of Tom's deep and wide-ranging knowledge.

In 1952, he became a Councillor, representing Dunrossness North. For three years, from 1960 to 1963, he was Convener of the Council. His advocacy of a study of the Faroese economy laid a basis for Shetland thinking for many years. As a member of the Museum committees, he was able to guide museum developments in a way that led to the erection of a modern museum building in Lerwick. The fact that it is now bursting at the seams is a further tribute to Tom's energy, for in 1964 he became first curator of the new museum. During the fourteen years of his curatorship, he built up the collections and gave the museum an international reputation.

It is a mark of the respect in which he was generally held that in 1976 the Secretary of State appointed him a Trustee of the National Museum of Antiquities of Scotland. He was also a member of the Treasure Trove Panel, which advises the Queen's and Lord Treasurer's Remembrancer on items claimed by the Crown in Scotland.

With the co-operation of Mrs Henderson, we are presenting Tom's story of 'The Wreck of the *Lastdrager*', one of the many manuscripts that he left behind him. It is an excellent expression of his love for the sea and its story.

The Wreck of the *Lastdrager*

T Henderson

Three tall ships came sailing forth together from the River Vliet, clearing from the Texel on a November morning, bound for Eastern seas. Newly overhauled from trucks to keel, gay with fresh paint, the morning sun drew bright glints from the profuse gilding about their high sterns, and the polished brass guns on their quarterdeck picked out the colours of pennants and the ensigns of the Free Provinces blowing out bravely at their flagstaffs. Three ships deep laden with all the products of Europe which canny Dutch merchants judged would find a ready market in those distant Dutch possessions beyond the seas. An assortment, surely, in the three cargoes: bales of cloth and hides of leather, casks of brandy and geneva, butts of wine and sack, pigs of lead and mercury in jars, clothes, boots, gunpowder, glassware, rope and canvas and Stockholm tar – the list is endless. And, most valuable of all, they carried treasure, specie, broad silver emblazoned with the armoured rider and the proud lion of the Provinces, thin gold ducats bearing a warrior, sword aloft and a sheaf of arrows gripped in his left hand; for coined money was the lifeblood of Dutch trade in the East Indies, and without regular injections from home that trade could not continue.

Two of the ships were of the standard type of East Indiamen called *fluijts*, evolved in Holland during the previous fifty years. Stout comfortable vessels, a broad beam tumbling home to a much narrower deck, lofty stern-castles with elaborate galleries embellished with much carving. Clumsy they might look to modern eyes, yet they were designed for the long voyages of their trade with an eye to seaworthiness rather than speed. A few extra days made little difference to a passage which would last several months anyway, and was of little consequence compared to the ship's eventual safe arrival.

These two ships were the *Lastdrager* and the *Diamant*. The third vessel of the little squadron was the *Windhond*, and she was not a *fluijt* but a *jagt*, smaller and lighter, a type often used for the carrying of dispatches though she would be laden with cargo as well.

The three ships sailed early in November, 1652, bound in the first instance for Goeree Roads. Those were troublous times in the Narrow Seas. Britain and Holland, the two greatest maritime nations in the world at that time and nations which had so much in common, were at each other's throats in the stupid conflict known to historians as the First Dutch War. At Goeree a vast convoy of merchant shipping was gathering to be escorted down Channel by the whole Dutch war fleet under the command of Admiral Martin Tromp himself.

What a spectacle that convoy must have presented when it eventually got under weigh. Six hundred sail heaving up their anchors and making sail together, standing out to sea with Admiral Tromp in the *Brederode* proudly leading the van.

Safe they might be from the enemy, but over the weather no man has control. Almost immediately a gale fell upon them, scattering the ships and bringing many into imminent danger. Soon the three deep-laden Indiamen were in trouble and, three days out, they bore up together to return to Goeree. They would have done better to have kept the open sea. Coming down on the land on a pitch-dark morning and with the gale blowing hard, by miscalculation or recklessness they struck the sandbanks off the Land van Schouwen. Lighter and drawing less water than the other two, the *Windhond* scraped over and went clear but the other two stuck fast.

Daylight revealed to those on board the *Lastdrager* a melancholy scene. Not far away, the *Diamant* lay a hopeless wreck with a distress signal flying, an appeal for aid which they were powerless to give, for they were themselves in the utmost peril. The gale was blowing as hard as ever, a wild sea was running, and their ship was bumping heavily on the ground. It seemed certain that they must share the *Diamant*'s fate. But soon after dawn a tremendous sea broke on board over the stern, smashed the galleries and flooded the cabin and at the same time lifted them across the bank into deep water beyond.

The *Lastdrager* was by no means out of danger. Her crew had to get their anchors over quickly to avoid driving ashore on the main coast where they now saw the *Windhond* lying a total wreck. Moreover the ship was leaking like a basket after her night on the sand, and only continuous pumping kept her afloat. There could be no question of continuing the voyage without much repair, and when the gale broke she returned to the Texel. When the ship was off Camperduin, young Camphuys was sent ashore in one of the pilot boats to travel to Amsterdam by way of Alkmaar and there give the Directors of the Vereenigde Oostindische Compagnie (Dutch East-India Company) news of the loss of the other ships and of the condition of the *Lastdrager*.

After the beating she had sustained, bearing in mind the care which the Company took of their ships, one would have expected the Indiaman's cargo to have been discharged and the vessel careened on the hard where her bottom could be thoroughly checked. Mysteriously this did not happen. A later report in the *Holland Mercurius* (not always an entirely reliable source) credited Captain Muykens with preventing a thorough survey. According to the newspaper, Muykens had on board considerably more goods of his own than he was allowed to take as a private venture, a fact which must inevitably come to light if the cargo was discharged.

Be that as it may, the rather superficial repairs were sufficient to satisfy two Company's surveyors – but not, it seems, the *Lastdrager's* own crew. When she was nearly ready for sea, the river where she lay, froze over. Twenty of the best seamen on board cleared out ashore over the ice and could not be bribed to return by the promise of double wages. News of this quickly got about among the seafaring community of Amsterdam and it was found to be nearly impossible to replace the missing men. Those who did eventually ship were green and inexperienced, with scarcely a seaman amongst them.

Thaw came at the beginning of February, and the new hands were brought off by lighter on the 5th of the month. Camphuys rejoined at the same time, though he admits he did not much relish the voyage ahead. Four days later the *Lastdrager* sailed, accompanied this time by the *jagt Avenhoorn* belonging to the Chamber of Hoorn. This time the Indiaman had on board an even more valuable consignment of specie. Her share of the original shipment had amounted to 25,000 guilders. To

this had been added at least half what had been recovered from the wrecked *Diamant*, so that she carried at the lowest estimate 37,000 guilders and possibly a good deal more. Counting crew, passengers and soldiers, the ship had on board a complement of some 206 souls.

This time the voyage started auspiciously. Dutch seamen hated the *achter om* route north around Britain in winter, dreading the combination of short daylight and wild weather so often encountered off Shetland at that season of the year. Quite often this would prove to be the most hazardous part of their whole long voyage. So, when the *Lastdrager* and her consort passed Fair Isle – desolate and snow-covered – on their sixth day out from the Texel, the two crews congratulated themselves that the worst of the passage was behind them. In a few short weeks they would be down among the flying fish and the cold Northern winter forgotten.

Their joy was short-lived. That night a screaming south-easter fell upon them and it must have been then that the two ships separated, the *Avenhoorn* eventually arriving all well at the Cape of Good Hope. Not so the *Lastdrager*. Day after day the tempest blew and the ship, always hove-to, sagged away to leeward before it. Day after day of misery, the gale fanged with stinging hail showers and a cold that pierced men to the bone. The wretched green hands shipped at the Texel would not keep the deck and skulked below in their bunks.

On the 23rd of the month the ship was close to and her crew apparently sighted 'the grim islands of Fero', and on that day disaster almost overtook them. A great sea broke on board which carried away the long-boat, threw the ship on her beam-ends and left her half waterlogged. Had she not partly righted herself, the *Lastdrager* must have quickly foundered. All hands fell to pumping and baling like madmen. Even the *geeluis*, those miserable ones who had refused to stir hand or foot for days past, found – 'so sweet is life' – energy to toil with the rest.

Desperate men can achieve much when their lives are at stake, and eventually the pumps sucked and the ship was free of 'her intolerable burden of water'. About this time the wind must have hauled up to north-west. They wore the ship round on the other tack in the hope that the wind would finally carry them out of 'this dark and dismal climate', but still hove-to and with her helm lashed the poor *Lastdrager* drifted on, no man on board knew where. They had seen neither sun nor stars since they left Holland.

The climax came on the evening of 2nd March when

one of the pilots suddenly burst into the after cabin with the fearful news that the ship was close down on a wild and rocky coast, on a dead lee-shore and not half a mile off, and that all on board must expect to be in eternity within the hour.

Hopeless as was the case, they tried to work clear of the land. The helm was unlashed and the 'groote schoverzeil' (possibly the main-topsail) loosed. But the gale ripped the sail from the yard before it could be set and, as the ship fell off before the wind, an overtaking sea struck the rudder and the helm was shattered to pieces. One of the steersmen was thrown by the whipstaff against the bulwark and mortally hurt. And the *Lastdrager* crashed ashore bow first where great breakers roared high at the base of cliffs which, though they are not so very tall, seemed to the terrified castaways below to touch the very clouds.

Try to picture the scene which followed. There the poor ship lay gripped fast by the rocks which pierced her through, prey to the fierce rollers which pounced in out of the darkness to rip the length of her stranded hull. Spars crashing down; a mast breaking with a noise like a gun shot. The stupefying din of the raging surf and howling snow-laden gale, and the crunch and grind of shattering timbers. And piercing through and over that dreadful cacophony a higher, poignant note, the voices of poor souls on the threshold of death crying out in their terror and knowing not that they did so.

Even then, the doomed folk on board the *Lastdrager* were granted respite for a little while. She had struck on an ebbing tide and, as always, the force of the waves eased somewhat as the sea went back. At the same time, this circumstance hastened the end of the ship. Jammed hard aground forward, her after part was still afloat, and as the tide receded the wrenching of the breakers put an unfair strain on the tortured hull. Presently she parted amidships and the stern half washed out and disappeared.

Up to this point there seems to have been little loss of life. When the ship showed signs of breaking, those on board had crowded forward into and under the forecastle, a hapless mass of frightened humanity. Then the tide turned and the scene changed. It was now that the real nightmare began. As the flood made, the breakers regained their fury, each running higher than the last, tearing away more and more of the already shattered wreck, soon sweeping off screaming victims by the dozen.

Jan Camphuys seems to have kept his head remark-ably well among all this tumult. He remained on board the wreck as long as he dared, and it was with the whole fabric disintegrating beneath him that he finally stripped off his heavy outer clothing and gave himself to the sea. By this time the creek was a grinding, heaving mass of floating cargo and broken timber, in the midst of which people were struggling, screaming and drowning. Beaten and buffeted, clinging to his piece of wreck, the boy washed backwards and forwards for a while, the backwash keeping him off the shore while splintered wood tore the rest of his clothes from his body and gashed his naked skin, and the bitter cold soaked in to his very bones. Then a great wave heaved him and his float high and dry on the rocks and from somewhere he yet found strength to scramble clear of the sea. Mechanically he began to crawl upwards, falling and hurting himself still more, and only when he found grass under his hands did it penetrate his dazed mind that he had scaled the cliff. Then 'I kissed for joy the ground and raised my bleeding arms to Heaven, thanking the Father of Goodness for this mercy!'

But lying stark naked on the cliff top, with the snow melting on his flesh, Jan realised that he was far from being in safety. He must find shelter or die, and stumbling somehow to his feet he staggered off into the black night, not knowing where. Nor had he gone far when he tumbled headlong into a ug well, so deep that he could scarcely feel the bottom. That ludicrous accident almost finished the hurt and exhausted boy. It took every morsel of what resolution he had left to scramble out. Then borne on the wind he heard voices raised in lamentation, and crawling towards the sound, found a group of his fellow sufferers huddling together, bewailing the fact that they had escaped the sea to perish miserably of the cold in a black and empty land.

At this moment of utter despair a strange thing happened. For a mere second of time Camphuys thought he saw one or two sparks of fire blowing on the wind. The merest glimpse, so quickly come and gone, it could have been a delusion of the boy's dazed mind. But as they peered into the dark, suddenly sparks came again, increasing in number, and the poor sea-driven Dutchmen could scarcely believe their eyes. Such a little thing, yet for them at that moment spelling the difference between life and death. Those sparks from a peat fire bright in the stormy dark must have seemed to them a miracle from God.

Each staggering as best he might, they sought the source of this phenomenon and found quite close by a house, low and primitive, built of rough stone and roofed with turf, from the chimney of which the sparks were issuing.

The building had two occupants, an elderly man and a young boy, who stared fearfully at the strange company which came knocking at their door. As he admitted later, the old man thought them a troop of ghosts – drowned sailor men, perhaps, roused from watery graves by the storm and raging sea. Nor could he make aught of their babble in a foreign tongue, until a Scotsman among the castaways spoke to him and explained whence they came. From this point there was no more hesitation. Assured of their earthly identity and though his means were slight, the old man treated them with the open-handed kindness which has always been the lot of shipwrecked men in Shetland.

The house as they now saw was a smithy, and the only light came from a fire burning on the forge. This the old man stoked into a blaze while his son fetched water from the well – that same well, incidentally, in which Jan had so nearly perished a little while before. Then the two prepared from their own limited stores a hot meal for the castaways while they, poor wretches, crowded around the fire and tried to thaw the cold from their limbs. Later they learned from their host that they were in Shetland – more specifically the *Lastdrager* had struck the tip of the headland called Crussaness near Cullivoe, at the north end of the island of Yell.

Twenty-six men had survived the wreck, including not one officer. Only Jan Camphuys, young as he was, and the ship's gunner, Jan Reynierszoen, could claim to represent Dutch East India Company authority. The rest were a mixed bag, including a quarter-master, the sailmaker, the ship's drummer, a corporal and six soldiers. Not all were Dutch. In addition to the Scotsman, there were one or two Germans and Frenchmen. Hardly any had got ashore unscathed. The corporal was badly hurt and hardly expected to recover, while Camphuys himself was in bad shape.

They had been luckier than they knew in finding shelter. The old Shetland man now told them that there was not another house anywhere near. During the summer fishing season fish were dried at Crook's Ayre, a beach not far away, and the smithy and booth to which they had come was part of the outfit of the curing station. But from August to May the place was uninhabited. He was himself a blacksmith and, having been commissioned to make some ironwork for the local landlord, he had decided to do the job in the station

smithy. He had come there in the very early morning with the boy – who was his son – in order to be ready to start work with the first of the daylight. Blissfully unaware of the tragedy and horror being enacted so close by, their first act had been to light the forge fire and try the bellows, hence the blowing sparks which had saved the survivors' lives.

What their fate would have been had they not found shelter was made tragically clear when daylight allowed one or two of the shipwrecked men to visit the geo where the ship was lost. Not far from the house they found two of their mates clasped in each other's arms for mutual body heat which had still not been enough. The two had died of the cold within a few score yards of the refuge they had failed to find. The shore itself was a fearful sight. Piled high with wreckage and cargo, there were corpses everywhere, many mangled beyond recognition. Approximately one hundred and eighty people had died during those dreadful hours.

The morning was still young when the blacksmith returned, bringing his landlord and employer. Although Camphuys does not name this man in his narrative, his identity is certain from local sources. He was Ninian Neven, Laird of Scousburgh in Dunrossness and Windhouse in Yell, one of the best-known writers and public notaries in Shetland in his own day, whose signature survives on many contemporary documents. In addition to the Windhouse lands, Neven owned much property in the north of Yell, including Crussaness, where the ship was wrecked.

Already news of the wreck had spread, and local men were gathering to the scene. Neven immediately gave orders that before any salvage was begun the dead were to be gathered and decently buried. Moreover his tenants were to bring dry hay and straw to the Crussaness smithy for bedding on which the shipwrecked men could lie, if not elegantly at least in reasonable comfort. It says much for his power over his tenants that, with such tempting loot strewing the shore, both orders were instantly obeyed. Food also was brought for the unfortunate men.

Regrettably, those who had gone to the shore brought, back a keg of brandy, from which some of the party now proceeded to drink themselves insensible, to Jan Camphuys's utter disgust. The spirits which, he says, could have been a means of recovery for their wounds, were thus 'abused to a deadly poison and a provocation of the infinite goodness of god'.

So the day, spent by some 'in godless drunkenness'

and by many in pain and misery, drew to its close. Bedding was prepared and the men went to rest but few could sleep. They were stiffening up now and feeling their hurts. Moreover the shock of their experience was heavy upon them. The young bookkeeper lay wakeful the whole night through, his body racked with pain and his mind a jumble of strange thoughts, wearying for the dawn.

But the morning light revealed a far different scene from that of the previous day. The gale which had plagued them so long had ceased its roaring. Anyone familiar with the idiosyncrasies of Shetland weather in winter would guess that the wind had hauled northerly during the night and fallen light, probably with a nipping frost, so that there followed one of those rare mornings which in an island winter compensate for much that is drab and dreary. From the hill-top to the tide-line the land lay under a white mantle of snow, pure and unsullied, shimmering in the rays of the rising sun. To the young Dutchman who records the beauty of that morning it brought a lifting of the spirit.

The sea had gone down with the calming of the wind and now, for the first time, the shipwrecked men were able to get right down on the rocks where their ship was lost. They sought among the wreckage for whatever might prove useful but they were mainly concerned to find provisions and weapons. For the fact mentioned earlier must not be forgotten: that Britain and Holland were at total war and these poor lads were cast away in what was technically an enemy country.

While the nervous seamen were not in a position to know the fact, the Dutch war caused little concern in Shetland. Primarily, the conflict was between England and the Netherlands, and although the two crowns had been united for fifty years before the events chronicled here, Scotland and England did not still identify closely as one nation. And if this was the case in Edinburgh, how greatly more so was it away north in Shetland where island folk did not even regard themselves as being truly Scots. Far removed from the politics and crises of Westminster, much more real to Shetlanders than any squabble between nations was the centuries-old friendship with the jolly Dutch fishermen whose advent on the Shetland scene each summer was as regular as the turn of the season itself.

But the *Lastdrager's* men did not know the true situation and so they sought for weapons among the wreckage of their ship. Scattered here and there among the rocks they found several broadswords and one or two

muskets. There were provisions in plenty, and then towards evening they found something else, an item which was to be the bane of their existence during the rest of their stay in Shetland. Lodged in a crevice, battered but whole and with its seals intact, they discovered one of the chests of specie.

They were not the only salvors on the shore that day. News of the wreck had by this time spread far, and with the smoothing of the sea came boats from all over the north isles, intent on plunder, loading up with all kinds of wares, and overdoing it in some cases, for two loaded to the gunwales with ironwork and jars of mercury foundered on their way home and nine men were drowned.

Strange it is and a reflection on men's cupidity how often a find of treasure brings immediate trouble in its wake. So it was now. Scarcely had the Dutchmen brought their money chest up from the shore than a rumour reached their ears that certain envious individuals planned to raid them and carry off their find. Fortunately this would seem to have been no more than a rumour, though it caused them considerable trepidation and one or two waking nights.

Worse was to follow. If the first crisis was a storm in a tea-cup, the next was real enough and doubly dangerous in that it arose from within their own party.

Choosing a time when the gunner was absent, about five of the less reputable survivors cornered Camphuys and informed him that they were going to break open the chest and split the money amongst all hands, fair share and share for all and double shares for Jan and the gunner.

Completely taken aback, the young bookkeeper was at first speechless, but he then burst out in a vehement denial that this should happen. The money belonged to the Company which, wreck or no wreck, they were all bound by oath or affirmation loyally to serve. For his own part, said Camphuys, he would sooner die than break his given oath. Nor could argument move him from this uncompromising stand. The situation was a stalemate. All hands must be equally involved or such a matter could never remain a secret, and even the most reckless had no desire to face the vengeance of the Council of Seventeen when it became known in Holland that they had pirated the Company's treasure.

Tempers became heated and the quarrel took a sinister turn. 'Why', demanded one, 'do we not do away with this infernal pencil licker?' And another, drawing his knife, flourished the naked blade under the boy's nose. 'This I will turn around in your heart', he snarled.

It was at precisely this ugly moment that the gunner came through the doorway, entirely ignorant of what was afoot, and demanded to know the trouble. Eagerly the would-be looters outlined the same proposal they had put to Camphuys, apparently confident that the gunner would be on their side. But Reynierszoen would have none of it. Who, he demanded with a stern countenance of the party at large, were determined against honour and reason to do this thing, and who were still honest men and would stand loyal to their duty? At once there was a split in the ranks. Nine men sided with Camphuys and the gunner, leaving fourteen in opposition – for the poor corporal who had been so badly injured had been removed elsewhere for better care.

Which side struck the first blow we are not told. But a scuffle ensued, culminating in a furious fight. Jan Camphuys, though still far from fit, waded in with the rest, and smote away as hard as his weak strength would allow, and records with some wonderment that in the heat of the battle – 'on which hung my life and the Company's money chest' – he felt neither ache nor pain. In the end the faithful faction were completely victorious, the others tumbling over each other out through the doorway and fleeing away along the brae 'though nobody pursued them'. They took shelter in the small house where the sick corporal lay at some distance up on the hillside.

Needless to say, the victorious party were much on their guard thereafter, setting a watch each night, but for some days nothing fresh disturbed their peace. And shortly some of the rebels made overtures of reconciliation, each blaming the others for the trouble and alleging that they had been led astray by ringleaders. Camphuys and Reynierszoen had little faith in the sincerity of this repentance, believing that rascals were impelled more by fear and hunger than any true feelings of regret. Nevertheless they felt it wise not to abandon their erring shipmates entirely. To have them back in the common billet was unthinkable. Wisely, the two decided to separate the members of the disloyal party from each other, lodging them in various crofters' houses and paying for their food and lodging.

During all this while Ninian Neven had treated the shipwrecked men with consideration and kindness, proving in every respect their friend, as Jan Camphuys gratefully records. On several occasions he and the gunner had been guests at the laird's house. Neven, who had travelled much, spoke fluent Dutch, as did his daughter Bessie, and they commiserated, often with tears in their eyes, with the two on misfortunes and present predicament. Discussing how they were to be relieved, Neven made a pertinent suggestion. There was, he said, a certain shipmaster living at Laxfirth, owner of a small sloop with which he traded to Norway, Holland, and other places. Because of the war, this man was out of employment and his vessel laid up. It was likely that if he were offered sufficient payment, he might charter his ship to carry the castaways home to Holland. So the laird wrote a letter to the Laxfirth skipper and they waited impatiently for a reply.

Suddenly a fresh alarm developed. Neven came to the Dutchmen in considerable agitation to tell them that he had information of another raid being planned to relieve them of their treasure. The plotters this time were local but not, one suspects, crofters and fishermen. Rather, they would seem to have been a bunch of wild young bucks of the so-called better class of whom there were certainly several in the area and to whom such an escapade was an adventure not to be missed. Some of those had tried to persuade young Neven, the laird's son, to join in the plot, and the boy had promptly informed his father.

This time the threat was very serious. With the division in their own ranks, the loyal Dutchmen were only eleven in number and poorly armed to withstand a determined assault. They could only view the future with foreboding. But once again Neven came to their aid. Since the chest of money was the raiders' only objective, the laird proposed that immediately after dark he would send his son round with a boat and remove the treasure chest to his own residence where it could be secretly buried and lie in safety. Then, if the shipwrecked men were attacked, they would simply abandon their house where there was nothing else of value and seek safety in the darkness.

This was duly carried out as soon as darkness fell and the Dutchmen breathed more freely, but they still set a night watch as they had done every night since the quarrel among themselves. About midnight the sentry spotted a man running desperately towards the house and instantly gave the alarm and all hands turned out quickly and seized their arms. But the stranger proved to be one of their own men, a badly frightened soldier, even more terrified by the warlike reception of his own comrades.

This man and five others had been living in a small

building up on the hill. Wakening in the night and looking out, he had discovered the house to be surrounded by armed strangers and had promptly made a dash for freedom. Someone fired a gun after him, the ball whistling past his ear. There could be no doubt, said he, that his companions had been slain to a man. On the strength of this highly alarming report Camphuys's men stood to their arms all night, but nothing further happened.

The outcome proved something of an anti-climax. In fact, the whole affair seems to have been a half-hearted and ill-managed prank rather than a serious attack on the Dutchmen. They discovered next morning that following the escape of the soldier and realising that the alarm must be given, the bold robbers had withdrawn without doing harm to anyone. Say Camphuys, '. . . these rogues, perceiving that their attempt had been discovered, returned before day and dew over an inland waterway to their dwellings and robbers' nests'. The island waterway was probably Basta Voe and from other evidence than Camphuy's narrative, one suspects that some of these amateur pirates hailed from Hascosay.

On 15th March came the eagerly awaited reply to Neven's letter to the Laxfirth skipper. It was disappointing. The man refused to convey them to Holland for any remuneration at all. It was more than his life was worth, he said. Should he be caught by the English on such an errand, with the war then raging he would assuredly be hanged as a traitor to the state. But he put forward an alternative proposal. He would sell them a small sloop, adequate to carry all their party for the short voyage, and they could sail themselves home. He invited them to come to Laxfirth and inspect the vessel.

Not what they had wished but a reasonable solution still. It is obvious that by this time they had opened the first treasure chest — from what other source could they have paid the crofters who were lodging their men? — and being thus in funds, buying the sloop was a practical proposition. By mutual agreement the gunner was the man best qualified to judge the condition of the ship and he set off for Laxfirth at once.

After all these nocturnal alarms the following day was fine, and for the meantime the castaways were relieved of some of their nervousness. After the fiasco of the previous night, no other threat loomed meantime on their horizon. Bored with having nothing to do, some of the men went fishing from the rocks where the ship was lost. The tide was out farther than usual, the bottom of a

March stream ebb, and rocks exposed farther out than they had ever seen before. Poking among the crevices, one presently found another chest of money lying in a cleft which had sheltered it from the breakers.

If in Camphuys's narrative one detects a slight lack of enthusiasm over this latest find, that is perhaps understandable. They only kept the thing in the house overnight, and on the following day it was secretly conveyed to the laird's house and hidden alongside the first.

Reynierszoen returned on the 24th and reported that he had examined the small vessel and in his opinion she was quite able for the short voyage. The owner was perfectly willing to sell. So, wasting no time, Camphuys and the gunner set out once more, reaching Laxfirth on the 28th of the month.

Jan was less impressed by the appearance of the sloop — she was called the *Hunter* — than his comrade had been. The vessel was small and far from new. Moreover she was laid-up in a unrigged state and no laid-up ship looks her best. But to the castaway Dutch seamen she represented deliverance, and they agreed to buy the little *Hunter* for the sum of 1,500 guilders on condition that she was rigged-out ready for sea and some slight alterations were carried out on board.

While the sloop was being prepared they had an unexpected stroke of luck. News reached Laxfirth that a Dutch ship was in Buishaven — which, be it noted, was the Hollanders' name for Bressay Sound. Surely nothing could be more significant of the unreality of the First Dutch War in Shetland than this incident: an enemy merchantman calling along the harbour as though all was as it had been when the nations were at peace. But be that as it may, the ship's presence for Camphuys and Reynierszoen was a windfall. Hurrying to the port, they were welcomed by their countrymen and able to buy several necessities for their forthcoming voyage which otherwise they would have had to do without.

At last came the day, the 8th of April, when the sloop was ready for sea and the two Dutchmen sailed her proudly out of Laxfirth and north along the coast to Yell. Alas! They found that matters had gone badly in their absence. The whole place was in an uproar. 'A certain *Graaf*, a fugitive from England', as Camphuys describes him, had arrived in North Yell with 'sixty armed soldiers' and was tearing the whole district apart in quest of goods from the wrecked Indiaman.

The young bookkeeper's information was not entirely correct. This man was not a *Graaf*, nor was he a fugitive from England. He was James Keith, sometime laird of Benholm, and at this time the Earl of Morton's Governor of Orkney. Furthermore, he was an unmitigated scoundrel. What he was doing in Shetland at this time, whether he had arrived by chance, or whether, hearing of the rich wreck, he had come north for the pickings, is not clear. For whatever reason, he had turned up at Scalloway and gathered about him as tough a bunch of ruffians as were to be found in the isles. Almost forty years had gone by since the headsman had featly separated Earl Patrick Stuart from his head at the Mercat Cross in Edinburgh, and time had removed most of his actual followers. But some infamous breed which had followed in his train still infested the isles, and James Keith seems to have collected the lot. There was scarcely a native Shetland name among his gang, nor were they professional soldiers. Having broken into Scalloway Castle and armed themselves with pikes and muskets from the armoury there, they borrowed 'Sumburgh's great boat' and set off for Yell, to descend on the north part of the island like a swarm of locusts.

Helpless in the face of these marauders, the crofting folk could only stand by and watch their houses and outbuildings being ransacked and their poor possessions either smashed or carried away. So far Ninian Neven's household had escaped, but he was full of foreboding, sure that his turn was coming, and he advised the Dutchmen to remove their treasure on board their ship as soon as possible. It was brought off as soon as dark fell.

Later that same night came the thing the laird had feared. The manor house was surrounded, an attempted parley was ignored, and the attack began with a fusillade of musket shots. Both Neven and Bessie were wounded, in the laird's case quite severely, after which the house was entered and stripped to the bone. That goods from the wreck must have been in the building is a virtual certainty, but the looters were not content with these. Everything went: casks of ale, hams, salted mutton, personal possessions – even a locked chest of papers which surely must have been carried off in mistake for something of greater pecuniary value.

The Dutchmen witnessed all this in a fury of frustration, grieved to see their good friend so treated, but too weak in numbers and too ill-armed to do more than look on.

They had their own troubles. While Jan and the gunner had been away, another and more sinister plot among their own people had come to light. The ring-leaders – they were five in number – of the original insurrection had been suspiciously quiet and docile ever since, though the sincerity of their reformation was always open to doubts. Now it appeared that one day during the leader's absence the drummer, asleep in a house where those five malcontents were, had awakened in time to overhear them discussing a fresh conspiracy to seize the money chests. They would keep quiet until the sloop was at sea, then they would await their opportunity and seize the ship, 'dance the pencil-licker overboard' and any others who opposed them, and sail away to some remote place where they 'would drink their tribulation out of their hearts and make fair weather with the money'.

Being thus forewarned, Camphuys and Reynierszoen made their own preparations. Ever since the original quarrel the five conspirators had avoided the rest of the party and kept much on their own. Thus it was not difficult to smuggle the loyal men quietly on board the sloop during the hours of darkness, and on the morning of 12th April they tripped their anchor and 'gave the sails to the wind'. Seeing the vessel under weigh, the traitors came rowing boldly off in a shore boat, but while they were still at a distance those on board hailed and told them they were to be left behind. They could wait another opportunity of getting back to their homeland and themselves taste a little of what they had planned for others. After pulling futilely after the sloop for a while, the mutineers were forced to turn back to the land, but not without 'a frightful outburst of profanity'.

The first lap of the voyage was a short one. The wind being foul, they put into Doggershaven and lay there three days until there came a morning with a brisk fair breeze. Getting under weigh again, this time in earnest, with all her sails bravely drawing, the little *Hunter* quickly ran Sumburgh Head and Fitful below the horizon. One may safely assume that the shipwrecked men watched the Shetland hills sink from sight without any regrets.

Their passage was not all fair sailing. They encountered a hard gale with a tumultuous sea which put them in some dread for the safety of the crowded sloop. But small and old though she may have been, she was apparently seaworthy enough and survived the blow without damage. The wind did, however, drive them much to the northward of their proper course. When they eventually sighted land on the 19th of the month, some of those on board identified it as the island of Heligoland. By this time they were in need of fresh provisions, but the wind was still blowing fresh and they were too far to leeward to fetch the island harbour. They came to anchor and rode for two days until the wind eased, not without some danger for they were lying on rocky ground which is fatal to a hemp cable. Nothing carried away, and at last with a fine morning they stood into the island roads and obtained the provisions they needed.

Leaving Heligoland on the 23rd, two uneventful days later they arrived safely in the River Vlie, and on the following day dropped their anchor for the last time opposite the palisades of Amsterdam, Jan Camphuys's native city. They had saved nothing of their personal belongings − and in Camphuys's case not even what he wore − but they brought back to Holland some 16,000 guilders of the *Lastdrager's* lost treasure.

After such an inauspicious beginning, the resolute and gallant young bookkeeper sailed again for the East Indies in the *jagt Vergulde Draak* in 1654. He reached Batavia safely this time, to begin a long and distinguished career in the service of the Dutch East India Company, a career which reached its climax when, at the age of 50, he became Governor of the whole Dutch East Indies. History recalls him as the most humane and trustworthy Governor the Dutch colonies ever knew.

His friend and benefactor, poor Ninian Neven, robbed of his property and almost of his life, raised action in the court at Scalloway against James Keith and several others for damages and restitution of his property. Precognitions of evidence in the case survive, but the result of the trial is not at present known, though it may be significant that just at this time James Keith

fell from grace with his lord and master and was deprived of his office in Orkney. Ninian Neven died in 1662 and was succeeded in his estates by his son Gilbert.

And what of the *Lastdrager* herself? Time rolled on and memories faded of the events chronicled here. Some fifty years after the disaster a notable Shetland 'wrack man' of that day, Captain William Irvine, forerunner of modern treasure divers, made an attempt on the wreck of the Indiaman. It is certain that at least two other chests of specie, and probably three, similar to those recovered by the shipwrecked men themselves, remained unaccounted for, and these were undoubtedly Irvine's objective. His success was meagre. In a report to the Earl of Morton he speaks of his 'pitiful purchase' and lists two large and rusted anchors and a few other valueless items, but of the treasure he found only a very few loose coins.

Thereafter the grave of the *Lastdrager* was not disturbed again by men for more than three hundred years. Until in 1971 the well-known Belgian diver and maritime archaeologist, Dr. M. Robert Stenuit, after extensive research in Holland, came north to the island of Yell and found the wreck on his second dive. He had considerable success, recovering many interesting artifacts, but of the surviving treasure he found only some five hundred loose coins. Returning during the following summer, he carried out an extensive and detailed search, using the most sophisticated electronic equipment, in an attempt to locate the broken-off stern part of the ship. He was unsuccessful. Only the forces which control the swirling tides of Blue Mull Sound know where they threw away their battered plaything and where under wide acres of sand the last of the *Lastdrager's* treasure lies.

Wooden Tumbler Locks in Scotland and Beyond

A Fenton and C Hendry

The delight that ingenious contrivances give to the human mind is well demonstrated by wooden tumbler locks. Though they were hardly the best way of making a house or shed secure as a rule, nevertheless there was pleasure in making them, and a set of smooth-working tumblers would give much satisfaction.

Scholars, who sometimes find outlets for their intellectual curiosity through pens rather than tools, have been drawn to tumbler locks for over a century. Romilly Allen produced an early study (Allen XIV (1879-80), 149-62), and Lieutenant-General Pitt-Rivers, appointed first Inspector of Ancient Monuments in 1883, followed soon after (Pitt-Rivers 1883, 7-9). Interest has also been taken by scholars in other countries, and the aim of the present paper is to review the collection of wooden tumbler locks in the National Museum in the light of the increasingly wide pool of knowledge about them.

As with readily made tools such as rope-twisters for straw ropes or threshing flails, wooden tumbler locks were never centrally produced and distributed, though no doubt a good local maker would find his products sought after by neighbours. They were home-made, and so it could happen in some areas that users of such locks thought of them as personal or local peculiarities. In the North Atlantic there were Faroese who said the lock was a Faroese speciality. Others attached such curiosity value to it that they thought the Faroese had got it from the Turks, who came there in their ships (Joensen 1977: 1, 25). Similarly in the Danish island of Lyø, they were regarded as local inventions. As recently as 1960 two old men could make them, and examples were shown proudly to teachers of handicrafts who came visiting the island. At least one inhabitant considered that the principle of the Yale lock was based on it (Højrup 1960, 112). There is also a Faroese story that an American, inspired by the tumbler lock mechanism, applied the principle to a metal lock and patented it. A few years later, it is said, a Dutchman began to produce a similar lock, and the American took him to court for infringing his patent. He lost his case when the Dutchman exhibited a Faroese tumbler lock (Williamson 1948, 300). Yale's American lock was patented on 29th January, 1861 and 27th January 1865 (Allen XIV (1879-80), 155).

In spite of such views about local specialities, the fact remains that wooden tumbler locks have a wide distribution. British and Scandinavian writers have shown that they have been used in Sweden, Norway, Denmark, Scotland and the Faroe Islands; in parts of Finland, Estonia and North Russia; in Germany, Switzerland, Holland, Greece and Spain (whence they were carried to Mexico and Peru); in North Africa, Egypt and Mesopotamia. Examples in the New World, for example in Jamaica, are known to have been made by negroes, but the original pattern is more than likely to be due to migrant Scots (Allen 1879-80; Pitt-Rivers 1883, 9; Højrup 1960, 115-18; Joensen 1977:1, 26). To these areas can be added France (Alsace), Lithuania, Lapland, parts of the USSR (including Siberia and the territory of the Cheremiss), Poland, Hungary, the Ukraine, Armenia, Austria, the Alps, the Balkans (including Cyprus), the whole Mohammedan East, and Guiana in South America (having been taken there from Africa). They were said to have been very common in the Middle East, and were even painted and decorated with metal, and sold to tourists, in Damascus and Cairo (Moszyński I, (1967-68), 527-28; Viski 1931, 41-48; Kosa 1979, 67-68).

This geographical range includes two main forms: double-handed locks with solid bolts in North and East Europe, and one-handed locks with hollow bolts in South and Central Europe and elsewhere. The former have a bolt that is separated from the key by tumblers, which it is the task of the key to raise in order to release the bolt. Accordingly, two hands are required, one to press the key, and one to draw or close the bolt. The latter are so formed that the key is inserted into the bolt itself, so that the lock can be opened with one hand. The links between lock and bolt in African and Asian locks consist of a varying number of iron or of wooden pegs, as in examples from the Middle East in the collections of the National Museum (Table IV, 2-3), and in locks from the Sahara and from Egypt illustrated by Højrup (1960, 118-119). A writer on the Mzab area of the Sahara noted that what appeared to be 'murderous-looking clubs' hanging from the men's girdles were really their house keys, each consisting of 'a flat piece of wood about a foot long at the end of which is arranged a pattern of large nails'. To open the door, this was pushed into a deep slot that ran from the doorpost horizontally towards the centre of the door. It there met the bolt, on which there was a corresponding pattern of nail holes. If the patterns on the key and the bolt coincided, a slight pull would unlock the bolt. No two pieces of wood had the same patterns of nails (Bodley 1947, 146-47).

In Scotland, documentary evidence goes back to the first half of the eighteenth century. In Captain Burt's twentieth letter to his friend in London, he told how the locks of the Highlanders' doors were made of wood, and, 'by the Way, these Locks are contrived so artfully, by Notches made at unequal Distances within-side, that it is Impossible to open them with any Thing but the wooden Keys that belong to them'. He noted, however, that there would be no great difficulty in getting in through the wall of the hut (Burt (*c.* 1734) II (1974), 143). At the end of the century, it was noted that in the Western Hebrides they made neat wooden locks, both for doors and chests, though insufficient detail is given for us to be sure that these were tumbler locks (Buchanan 1793, 112). In 1824, Macculloch, who had read Captain Burt, also spoke of them, as a 'matter of luxury and not of necessity' (Macculloch III (1824), 195). The only other possibility so far noted is the reference to a 'slight wooden latch' to exclude cattle, as the only fastening on the house-doors of the parish of Glensheil in Ross-shire (NSA (1836), XIV (1845), 202), though this source may refer simply to latches and not to locks. There do not appear to be any special terms in Scots or Gaelic (*glas* = lock) that point to tumbler locks rather than to any other kind.

The richest source is the physical evidence of tumbler locks preserved in museum collections (Table, I-II, IV), the National Museum's collection being particularly good, and including comparable locks from other countries.

Table I. Scottish Tumbler Locks

(a) In National Museum of Antiquities of Scotland

	No./Neg.	*Date of Accession*	*Place of Origin*	*Description*	*Reference*
1.	MJ1, C10478	1860	Snizort, Skye	Double-sided: 6 tumblers	Allen 1879-80, 159-60; Catalogue 1892, 337
2.	MJ2, C10490, C5149	1833	North Ronaldsay, Orkney	One-sided; 4 tumblers. Bolt now missing	Allen 1879-80, 157-58; Catalogue 1892, 337-38
3.	MJ3, C10479	1863	North Ronaldsay, Orkney	One-sided; 3 tumblers. Bolt has 6 slots.	Catalogue 1892, 337
4.	MJ4, C5152	1878	St. Kilda	One-sided; 2 tumblers; wooden key with lifting pins of iron	Allen 1879-80, 158; Catalogue 1892, 338
5.	MJ201, C10476	1925	St. Kilda; got in 1883	Double-sided; 4 tumblers; key has copper pins	
6.	MJ212, C10484	1932	Scalloway, Shetland	One-sided; 3 tumblers	
7.	MJ250, C11402	—	St. Kilda; got in 1912	One-sided; 2 tumblers	
8.	MJ251, C11402	—	St. Kilda; got in 1912	One-sided; 2 tumblers	
9.	C11401	—	?St. Kilda	One-sided; 3 tumblers; base plate is part of barrel stave	
10.	C10486	—	Not known	Double-sided; 3 tumblers; key has metal pins	
11.	L.1967.32, C11402	Loan, 1967	St. Kilda	Bolt only; 2 tumblers; one-sided	
12.	C10475	Loan from Royal Scottish Museum	Not known	One-sided; 1 tumbler	
13.	C10487	—	Not known	Double-sided; 5 tumblers	
14.	C10489	—	Not known	One-sided; 2 tumblers	

(b) Tankerness House Museum, Kirkwall, Orkney

15.	—	1964	Conglebust, North Ronaldsay	One-sided	

(c) Highland Folk Museum

16.	C12853		St. Kilda	One-sided; 2 tumblers	Hay 1978, 125-27

(d) Glasgow Museums and Art Galleries

17.				Includes part of door	
18.				One-sided; 2 tumblers	

(e) From published sources

19.	C5151	1880	Harris	One-sided; 2 tumblers; key has two pins cut out in it	Allen 1879-80, 160
20.	C12854	1880	Harris	Double-sided; 2-limbed key	Allen 1879-80, 159
21.	'In the Patent Museum at South Kensington'. C12556(b)	1883	'Old Scottish'	One-sided; 2 tumblers	Pitt-Rivers 1883, 8, Plate I, Figs. 12A-17A
22.	Ibid. C12555(a)	1883	'Old Scottish'	Double-sided; 3 tumblers	Pitt-Rivers 1883, 8, Plate II, Figs. 18A-22A

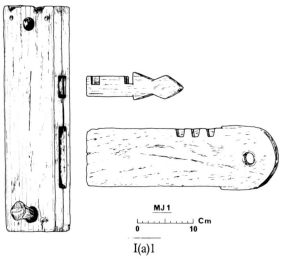

MJ 1

I(a)1

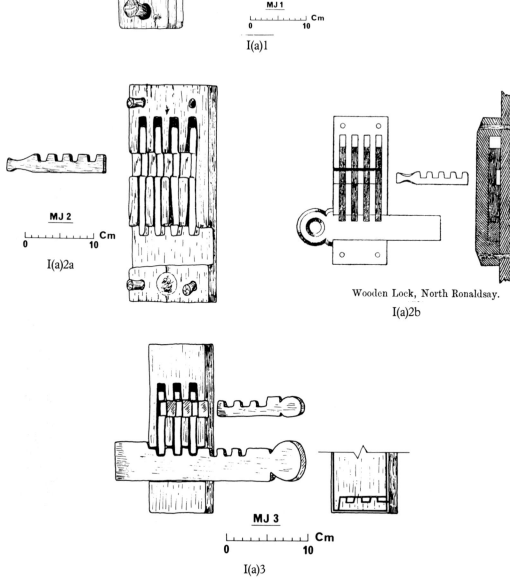

MJ 2

I(a)2a

Wooden Lock, North Ronaldsay.

I(a)2b

MJ 3

I(a)3

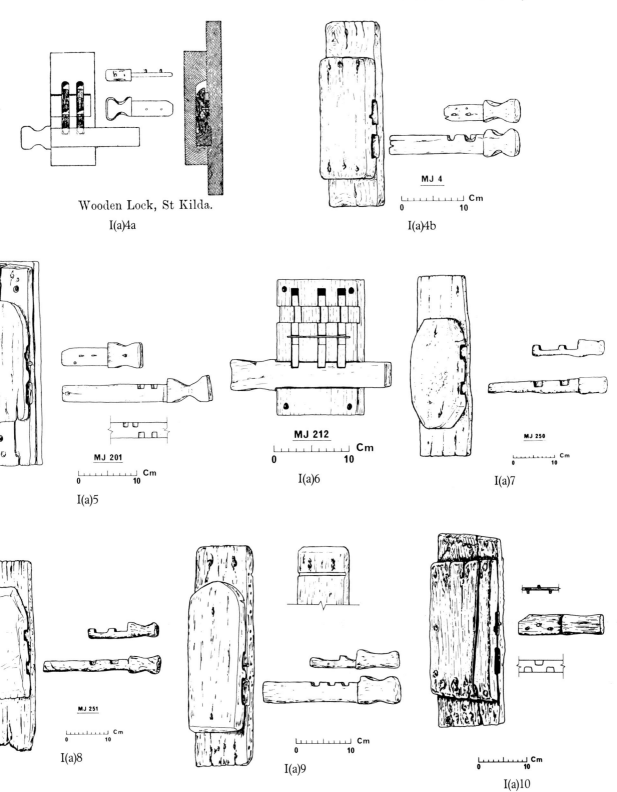

Wooden Lock, St Kilda.

I(a)4a

MJ 4

Cm

0   10

I(a)4b

MJ 201

Cm

0   10

I(a)5

MJ 212

Cm

0   10

I(a)6

MJ 250

Cm

0   10

I(a)7

MJ 251

Cm

0   10

I(a)8

Cm

0   10

I(a)9

Cm

0   10

I(a)10

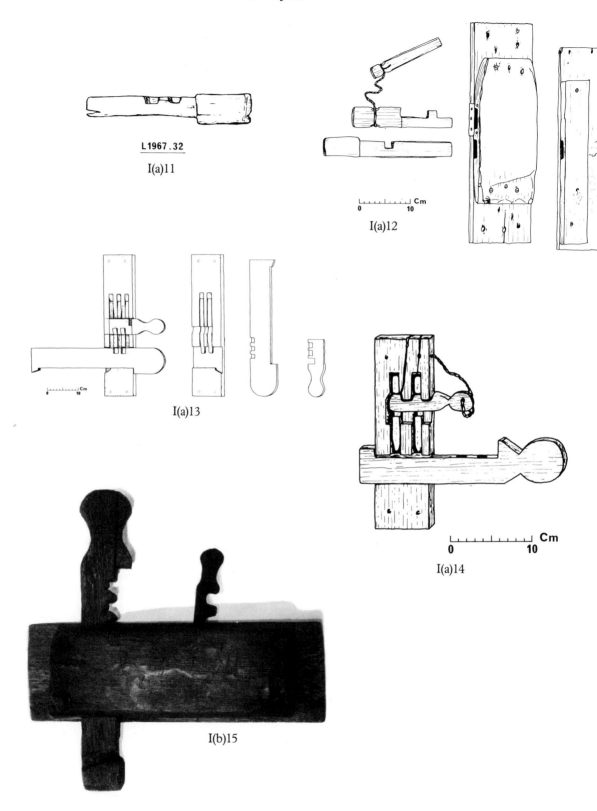

L1967.32

I(a)11

I(a)12

I(a)13

I(a)14

I(b)15

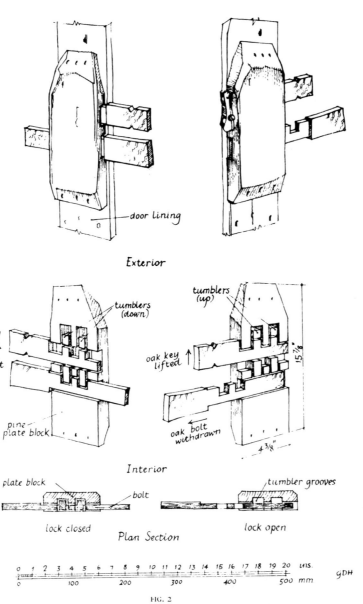

Exterior

Interior

Plan Section

FIG. 2

Wooden tumbler lock, Isle of St. Kilda, Scotland.

I(c)16

I(d)17

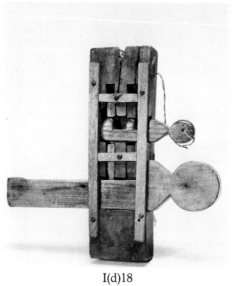

I(d)18

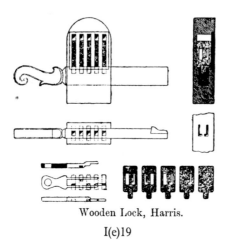

Wooden Lock, Harris.

I(e)19

Fig. 3. Wooden Lock, Harris.

I(e)20

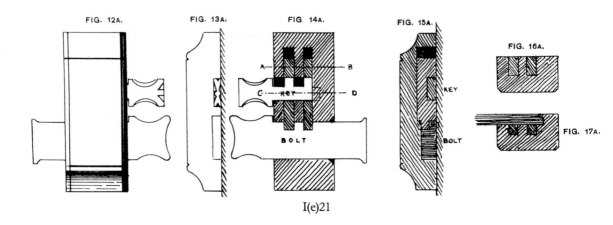

FIG. 12A.   FIG. 13A.   FIG. 14A.   FIG. 15A.   FIG. 16A.

FIG. 17A.

I(e)21

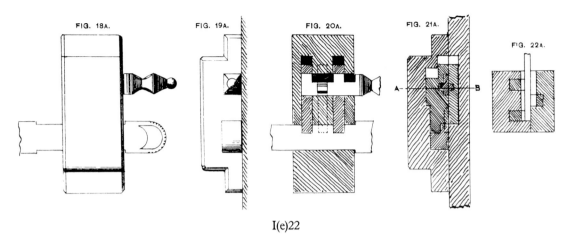

FIG. 18A.   FIG. 19A.   FIG. 20A.   FIG. 21A.   FIG. 22A.

A— —B

I(e)22

Table II. Northern Tumbler Locks

(a) In National Museum of Antiquities of Scotland

No./Neg.	Date of Accession	Place of Origin	Description	Reference
1. MK1, C10485	1882 Label: 'A. Cunningham Hay, Lerwick 1892'	Norway	One-sided; 3 tumblers	Catalogue 1892, 340
2. MK3, C10481	1882 'model'	Not known	3 tumblers	Catalogue 1892, 340
3. MK4, C10488	1882 'model'	Not known	1 tumbler	Catalogue 1892, 340
4. MJ176, C10480	1898 'model'	Faroe Islands	One-sided; 3 tumblers	

(b) From published sources

No./Neg.	Date of Accession	Place of Origin	Description	Reference
5. C11925	1781-82	Faroe Islands	Double-sided; 4 tumblers; key has flat pins, 2 on each side	Svabo (1781-82), 1976, facing 270.
6. C12556(a)	1883	Faroe Islands	'Double tumbler lock'	Pitt-Rivers 1883, Plate I, Figs. 9A-11A
7. C11404		Faroe Islands, Lamhauge	Double-sided; 4 tumblers	Joensen 1977, 25
8-9. C11406		Faroe Islands	Left one said to be over 200 years old	Joensen 1977, 29
10. C12555(b)		Norway	3 tumblers	Pitt-Rivers 1883, Plate II, Figs. 23A-25A
11. C11405		Norway, Rauland	Mechanism sketched from another example in Norwegian Folk Museum; 3 tumblers	KLNM XI (1966), 58; also Joensen 1977, 27
12. C12592		Denmark, Lohals, Langeland	3 tumblers, with through-passing key	Højrup 1960, 115
13. C12593		Denmark, Vindeby	2 tumblers	Højrup 1960, 114

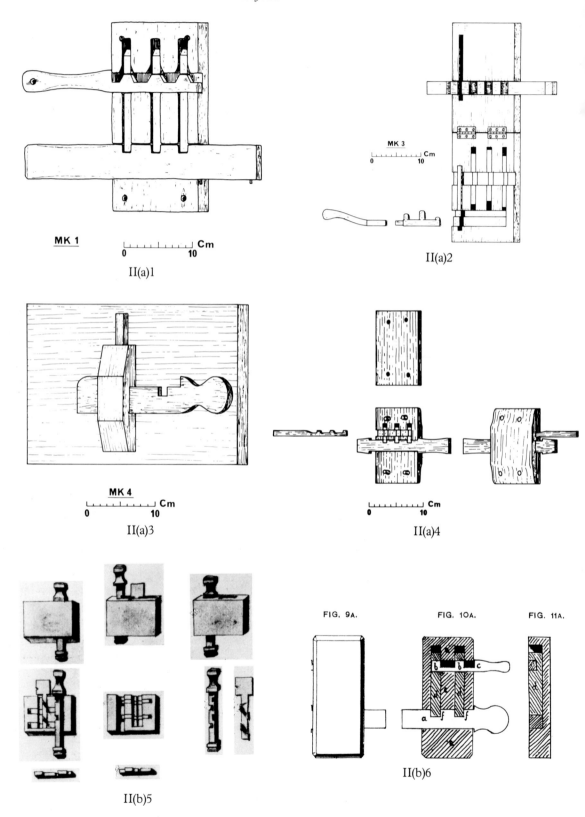

MK 1

0 ———————— 10 Cm

II(a)1

MK 3

0 ———— 10 Cm

II(a)2

MK 4

0 ———————— 10 Cm

II(a)3

0 ———————— 10 Cm

II(a)4

II(b)5

FIG. 9A.   FIG. 10A.   FIG. 11A.

II(b)6

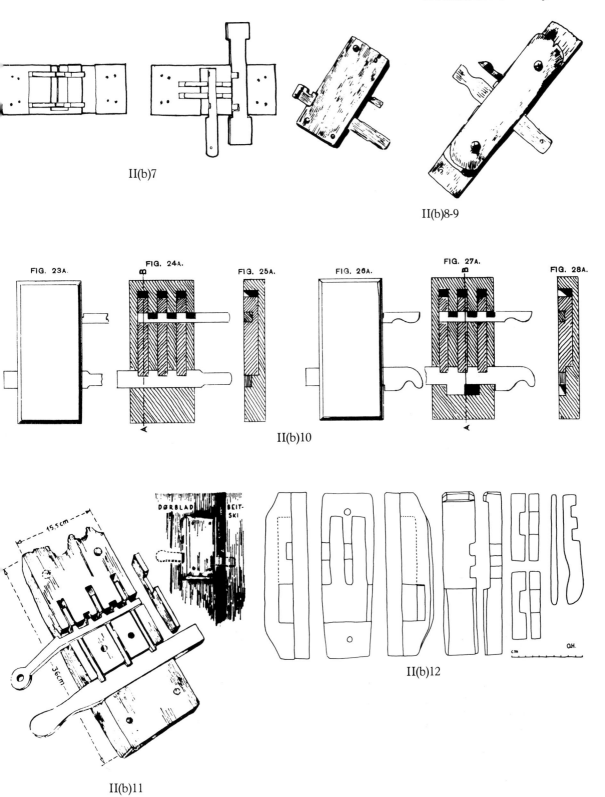

II(b)7

II(b)8-9

FIG. 23A. FIG. 24A. FIG. 25A. FIG. 26A. FIG. 27A. FIG. 28A.

II(b)10

DØRBLAD BEIT-SKI

II(b)11

II(b)12

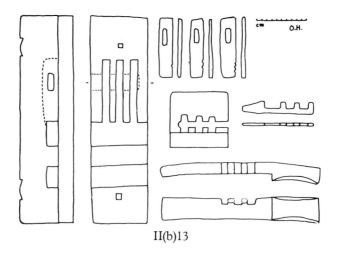

II(b)13

Table III. Jamaica and British Guiana (from published sources)

No./Neg.	Date of Accession	Place of Origin	Description	Reference
1. C12555(c)		Jamaica	'Made by negroes'; 3 tumblers	Pitt-Rivers 1883, Plate II, Figs. 26A-28A
2. C12555(d)		British Guiana	2 tumblers	Pitt-Rivers 1883, Plate II, Figs. 29A-31A

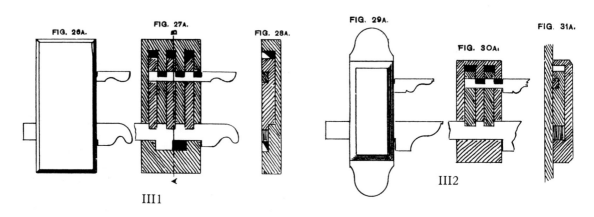

III1   III2

Table IV. Other Tumbler Locks
In National Museum of Antiquities of Scotland

No./Neg.	Date of Accession	Place of Origin	Description	Reference
1. C10477	1909 'Presented by Mr Curle'	—	2 tumblers; bolt can be pulled by thong. Special key (missing) at right angles to bolt.	—
2. MK2, C10491	1882, 'model'	Persia	Two-pin key	Catalogue 1892, 340
3. C10482	1981	Middle East	Four-pin key	

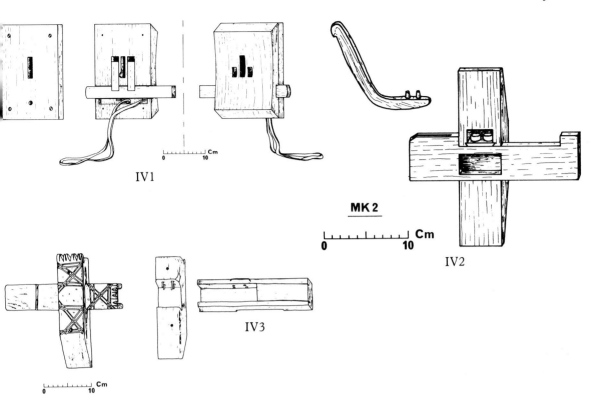

IV1

MK 2

IV2

IV3

Table V. Central Europe (from published sources)

No./Neg.	Date of Accession	Place of Origin	Description	Reference
1. C12559	—	Poland. In Ethnographic Museum, Kraków		Moszyński; I (1967), 527, Fig. 459, 3
2. C12558	—	Hungary	Double-sided	Magyar Néprajzi Lexikon 2 (1979), 67
3. C12557	—	Hungary	In position	Ibid. 68
4. C12598	—	Hungary	Two-tumbler, bolt missing	Viski 1931, 43, Fig. I, 5
5. C12597	—	Hungary	Three-tumbler, open and closed. Key enters same opening as bolt	Ibid. 45, Fig. II, 9-10
6. C12596	—	Hungary	Key enters bolt of lock	Ibid. 45, Fig. II, 13
7. C12595	—	Hungary	Four-tumbler	Ibid. 47, Fig. III, 14
8. C12594	—	Hungary	Three-tumbler, lying diagonally across bolt	Ibid. 53, Fig. V, 29-32

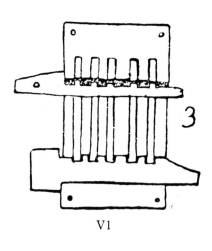

V1

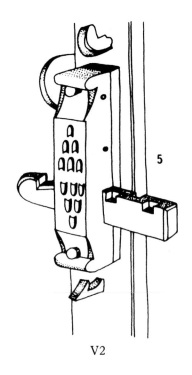

V2

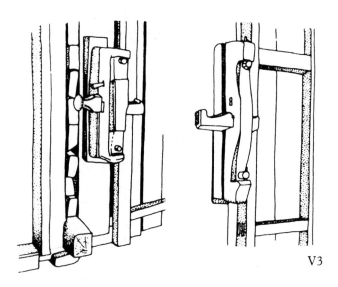

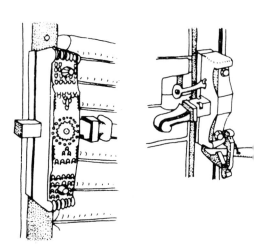

V3

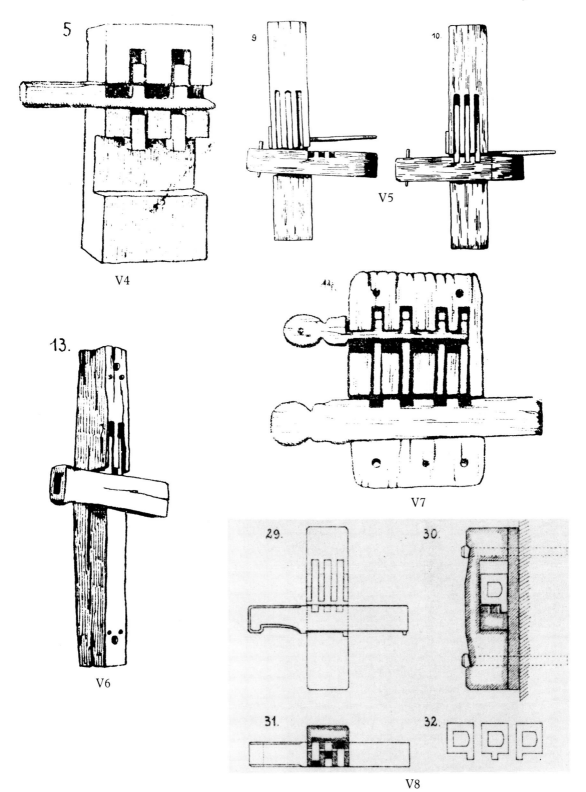

V4

V5

V6

V7

V8

The Scottish locks are of one basic pattern, but vary in the number of tumblers and the forms of linkage between lock, tumblers, and bolt. They consist of two rectangles of wood fixed together, in some cases by means of wooden dowel pegs. The inside is hollowed to allow the tumbler mechanism to work. The long side has a larger opening for the bolt, and a smaller one for the key. For simpler locks, only one side of the sandwich is hollowed out (e.g. Table I, 2, 6). One of the simplest is in Table I, 12, which appears to have only one tumbler, though in external appearance it is no less substantial than any others.

Tumblers appear to range in number from one to six. Locks with tumblers numbering up to four may be one-sided; but for greater numbers, and for numbers from three and upwards, they are more likely to be double-sided internally. As Romilly Allen noted a century ago, the six-tumbler lock from Snizort, Skye (Table I, 1), is in essence two locks set face to face, with the bolt between them (Allen 1879-80, 160). In this case, the bolt has to have sets of notches at each side, and they must be differently spaced on each side. For the key to work, it must also be double-sided. It may have sets of notches on each side, or it may be provided with wooden pegs or iron pins at one or both sides, according as the lock is single- or double-sided (Table I, 4, 5, 10).

The principle of use is straightforward. The tumblers move in vertical grooves. To open or close the bolt, the key is inserted so that its pegs or notches engage with the tumblers. It is not turned, but lifted, to draw the tumbler tongues out of the notches in the bolt. The freed bolt may be moved back or fore by the operator's other hand. When the key is taken out, the tumblers keep their place in the bolt by their own weight. It is easy enough to understand, therefore, that if such locks were on outer doors, moisture could cause the wood to swell so that the mechanism would jam (Hay, 12 (1978), 127).

The greatest degree of sophistication so far noted is in a lock from Harris, described in 1880 (Table I, 19). The key was double, and there were single tumblers lifted alternately by each of the legs of the key. Each tumbler had two openings, one rectangular and one L-shaped. The key had to pass through the rectangular opening to lift the tumbler beyond. The L-shaped opening allowed the projecting tooth on the inside of the key to catch the lower under-part of the L, and lift the tumbler. The system would work if both openings

were L-shaped, but the rectangular form prevented a key with lifting catches on the opposite side from opening it. The key twisted at the end in order to get into the farthest of the five tumblers, as an anti-picking device (Allen, XIV (1879-80), 160).

Norwegian, Danish and Faroese tumbler locks are broadly parallel to those known from the north and west of Scotland. Insofar as evidence is available, Norwegian locks, *spilalås*, are one-sided, with three tumblers (Table II, 1). The number of tumblers can vary, but there is no indication that there are two-sided forms (KLNM XI, 58), though a survey of Norwegian locks might well show that they existed. A Norwegian example in the 'Hazelius Museum', Stockholm, drawn in 1883, is one-sided, with three tumblers (Pitt-Rivers 1883, 8).

In the Faroes, however, double-sided locks are known from the earliest known illustration of tumbler locks in 1781-2 (Table II, 5). No supporting description is given, though the locks relate to a section of the book that deals with outhouses, but the drawings are clear enough. There are four tumblers in a double-sided lock, spaced two by two on each side of the bolt. The key is fitted with flat pins, two on each side, for raising the tumblers. This form continued, for a lock of presumably later date, from Lamhauge, has a comparable mechanism (Table II, 7). There is also a three-tumbler example with an iron key (Højrup 1960, 116). Simpler forms co-existed, however, as shown by a Faroese example in the National Museum (Table II, 4), which is one-sided with three tumblers.

The matter of double-sidedness raises an intriguing question. It is known in the Faroe Islands from the late eighteenth century. In Scotland, there is the six-tumbler example from Snizort (Table I, 1), one from St. Kilda (Table I, 5) and two unlocalised examples, one with six, and one with three, tumblers (Table I, 10, 13). A Scottish double-sided lock with three tumblers was illustrated in 1883 (Pitt-Rivers 1883, 8). Double-sidedness, therefore, is a feature shared by Scotland and the Faroe Islands. It may be one of the numerous aspects that mark a degree of cultural cohesion in the countries of the North Atlantic as a development independent of the Norwegian homeland (cf. Fenton 1980, 5-16).

This question must be tested by further future examination of tumbler locks in Norway or elsewhere in the Scandinavian peninsula, though a study carried out in 1960 may indicate that the picture as now out-lined may not be greatly changed. Danish examples recorded by Højrup are, as for Norway, one-sided, though a large gate-lock from Vindeby on Tåsinge differs from all others noted so far in having an arrangement whereby the key has to pass right through apertures in the tumblers which have to be made wide enough for this way of working (Højrup 1960, 113, 119). Højrup considers this to be a local development, but it is relevant to point to one Hungarian example in which the three tumblers lie diagonally, two straddling the bolt and one passing through an opening cut into it (Table V, 8). The range of variation, clearly, owes a good deal to local ingenuity. It is not too difficult to imagine that in some instances similar or comparable means of making the mechanism effective could have been invented separately in different areas.

Tumbler locks are not only to be found in Northern Europe and places in the Southern Hemisphere to which Northern European influences have spread, however. As long ago as 1929, the Polish ethnologist Kazimierz Moszyński drew attention to what he called 'blind' locks (presumably because they had no keyhole in front) and to their wide distribution in Europe, Africa and Asia. They were known almost everywhere among the Slavs, in Bulgaria, and in parts of Russia, though not in Polesia or White Russia. Even then they were going out of common use. Moszyński believed that the wooden tumbler lock of this type was the more primitive, because of its occurrence in peripheral and relict areas. He illustrated an example with five tumblers preserved in the Ethnographic Museum in Kraków (Table V, 1). The present writer noted a wooden tumbler lock in the Kolómenskaya Museum, on the edge of Moscow, in October 1982.

Wooden tumbler locks are also known in Hungary. The *fazár*, wooden lock, was widely used in the towns and villages, and was home-made. Sometimes it was neatly carved and decorated with patterns of geometrical shapes. As for similar locks in Northern Europe, it was gravity operated, the tumblers falling into the slots in the bolt by their own weight.

The number of tumblers varied, as elsewhere, and the number of teeth in the keys varied to match. The opening for the key could be in one of three positions: above that for the bolt, and separate from it, as in the tumbler locks of the north; as part of the same open-ing as for the bolt, which was made deep enough to give room for bolt and key together; or in the open end of the bolt itself, so matching the one-handed locks of the south, though in other respects the mechanism resembled those of the north. Hungarian and Transylvanian tumbler locks thus appear to indicate that here in the Carpathian basin there was a meeting and mingling of the one-handed and double-handed forms of tumbler locks, at a point of linkage of two wide cultural zones of the world (Viski 1931, 41-48; Koza 1979, 67-68).

The broadening of the known distribution as indicated above means that Scandinavia can no longer be considered as the headquarters of double-handed tumbler locks, even if it is at least possible that they were known to the Vikings (cf. Joensen 1977:1, 28). They were, at least, known in the Middle Ages in Scandinavia (KLNM XI (1966), 58). They are a very much more widespread phenomenon, for which the point of origin, if there is one, must lie elsewhere, and Pitt-Rivers turns out to be fully justified in making the comment:

> I see no reason to suppose that this class of lock was confined to Scotland or to Scandinavia. They may probably have existed in other parts of Europe, where, being made entirely of wood, they have long since decayed, and their representations may have survived only on the outskirts of civilisation (Pitt-Rivers 1883, 8).

Though neither Lowland Scots nor Gaelic has special names for tumbler locks, there is a little more variety elsewhere. Norwegian *spilalås* indicates a lock (*lås*) with wooden 'splints' (KLNM XI (1966), 60). In the Island of Lyø in Denmark, a two-tumbler lock is a *halvlås*, 'half-lock', whilst one with three tumblers is a *hellås*, 'whole lock', which is more secure (Højrup 1960, 112). In the Faroe Islands, the name is *kvølpalaas* (Svabo (1781-82), 1976, facing 270), and in Modern Faroese *hvølpalás*. This was glossed around 1800 as 'sera lignea, quam claudunt paxilli lignei in obicem cadentes' (wooden lock, closed by wooden tumblers falling into the bolt), and *kvølpur* as 'pessulus serae ligneæ' (pin of a wooden lock). The Icelandic equivalent was said to be *hvolpalás* (Svabo, I (1966), 463), but Icelandic colleagues, Professor Herman Pálsson of Edinburgh University, and Dr. Thor Magnusson, Director of the National Museum of Iceland, have been unable to find any supporting Icelandic evidence. The Hungarian name, *fazár*, 'wooden lock', is qualified by the adjective *makkos*, literally 'acorned', but this is a learned translation of the Greek *βάλἄνος* which means either an acorn, or a pin that held the bar or bolt of the door in place. Apart from the Danish terms which indicate value judgements for different degrees of complexity, the terms simply indicate the sliding or dropping motion of the tumblers.

References

Allen, J Romilly — Notes on Wooden Tumbler Locks, in *PSAS* XIV (1879-80), 149-162

Berg, A, Christensen, Jnr, A E and Liestøl, A — Lås, in *KLNM* XI (1966), 48-61

Bodley, R V C — *Wind in the Sahara* London 1947

Buchanan, J L — *Travels in the Western Hebrides* London 1793

Burt, Captain — *Letters from a Gentleman in the North of Scotland to His Friend in London* (c. 1734) Edinburgh 1974. 2 Vol.

Catalogue — *Catalogue of the National Museum of Antiquities of Scotland* Edinburgh 1892

Fenton, A — Northern Links, in *Northern Studies* 1980:16, 5-16

Hay, G D — Scottish Wooden Tumbler Locks, in *Post-Medieval Archaeology* 12 (1978), 125-127

Højrup, O — Lås af træ, in Stoklund, B, ed. *Folkeliv og Kulturlevn. Studier tilegnet Kai Uldall 14. september 1960* (Nationalmuseet) 110-124

Joensen, J P — Eitt Sindur um Hvølpalásið, in *Mondul* 1977:1, 25-29

KLNM — *Kulturhistorisk Leksikon for nordisk Middelalder*

Kosa, L — Fazár, in *Magyar Néprajzi Lexikon* II (1979), 67-8

Macculloch, J — *The Highlands and Western Isles of Scotland* London 1824. 4 Vols.

Moszyński, K — *Kultura Ludowa Słowian* Warszawa 1967-68

NSA — *New (Second) Statistical Account*

Pitt-Rivers, Lt-Gen — *On the Development and Distribution of Primitive Locks and Keys* London 1883

PSAS — *Proceedings of the Society of Antiquaries of Scotland*

Svabo, J C — *Indberetninger fra en Reise i Færøe 1781 og 1782* (ed. Djurhuus, N) København 1976

Svabo, J C — *Dictionarium Faeroense Faerøsk-dansk-latinsk ordbog* Vol. I. København 1966

Viski, K — Makkos fazáraink, in *Néprajzi Ertesítöje* XXIII/2 (1931), 41-55

Williamson, K — *The Atlantic Islands. A Study of the Faeroe Life and Scene* London 1948 (new edition London 1970)

Lewis Shielings

D Macdonald

In a popular Lewis song reference is made to the fact that it was a long-established custom in the Island to send cattle to the shielings (*airighean*), on the completion of the croft work in spring and cutting of the peats. When this custom of sending cattle away to distant pastures during the summer months originated is unknown, but it was in the distant past. It was common, not only throughout the Western Isles but also on the Scottish mainland.

There are still shielings in Norway, where they are called *sæters*, and during the centuries when Lewis was occupied by the Norse they gave this name, Gaelicised as *shader*, to many places. There are about thirty 'shaders' in Lewis, such as Grimshader, Guershader, Linshader and Carishader.

The amount of arable land was always very limited, with the result that mortality among stock was high during the winter and spring. Yet cows were essential, for their sale helped to pay rents which could be in kind as well as cash. It was to get the animals fit to stand the winter scarcity of fodder better and to provide butter and cheese also, for sale or for home consumption, that this annual migration with stock was so important. It seemed that the fat content of milk from cows which grazed on the coarse moorland grasses was much higher than that got from those which fed on finer pastures.

In order to keep the outrun outside the dykes surrounding the crofts for the use of animals during the autumn, winter and spring, when the further pastures were too boggy even for the small, light Hebridean cattle, all animals had to be sent at least three miles beyond the village dykes during the summer months. Black turf dykes in many areas still remind one of the boundary between the outrun and the shieling pastures. Any animal which could not be sent away had to be tethered on the owner's croft.

Each village had its own shieling sites. Some were by lochs, some in glens and some even on hillsides.

They all had easy access to running water to keep the dairy utensils clean.

Some shielings were known by the owner's name, such as Airigh Dhomhnuill Chaim, Airigh an Tailleir; grouped shielings were referred to by their location, for example Airighean Loch Sgarasdail, Airighean Dhibiodail, Airighean Loch an Eilein or Airighean Roineabhal. Others had names like Airigh na Gaoithe (Windy Shieling), Airigh no h-Aon Oidhche (One Night Shieling), and Airigh Fad As (Distant Shieling).

Of the three types of shieling in Lewis the oldest, and most enduring, was the 'both', which was built wholly of stones, with a thick covering of turf to keep it wind and weatherproof. It resembled an old beehive skep or an Eskimo igloo. There were only three openings in its corbelled walls, two doors, some distance apart, each about 3ft. in height and 2ft. wide, the windward one of which was always closed, and a smokehole (*fàrlas*) at its apex, about a foot in diameter, which could be closed by a flat stone or a piece of turf in inclement weather. This hole, along with the doors, admitted some light into the 'both' along with the smokehole and allowed egress for the smoke, when it so wished.

The floor in this circular building was about 10 to 12 ft. in diameter and the height to the smokehole from 6 to 7 ft.

The fireplace could be midfloor, but it was usually placed between the two doors, while an upraised, wide, stone platform was made directly opposite it to serve as a bed, and when necessary as a table. A stone coping, covered with dry turf, fronted the bed. It was called the *cailleach* or old woman, and formed an excellent seat. Two other stone benches ran from each side of the bed to the respective doors. Recesses in the walls served as depositories for milk basins and provisions.

The second type of shieling, the *airigh*, was rectangular in shape, and approximately 12 ft. long by 10 ft. wide, with a low roof thatched with over-lapping turf slabs about 3 ft. by 2 ft., laid on a slight framework of timber which stretched from the ridge-pole to the wall tops. The fireplace was placed against an end wall, facing the bed platform, with the smoke-hole directly above it. The ridge-pole halved this opening, and this allowed the windward section to be closed with turf when necessary.

The interior arrangements were similar to those in the 'both'. It used to have two doors, but later shielings had only one. The walls were about 3 ft. thick, with the inner surfaces of stone and the outer ones of turf or alternate layers of stone and turf.

The third type, the Spring House (*Tigh Earraich*), was an exact replica of the blackhouses which were so common towards the end of the last century. Both humans and animals were housed under the one roof. It was as if a byre portion had been added to an ordinary shieling, for the use of the milch cows and calves during cold, wet nights, or during those periods of scarcity when fodder was scarce in late spring and the only recourse was to send the cows out to the summer pastures earlier than usual, where they could get some heather to eat.

The domestic section of this dwelling was practi-cally the same as that in the *airigh*, except that the fireplace was midfloor, and that there was no partition between it and the byre. The animals seemed quite content with this arrangement and the warmth from the fire and human companionship. Later a wall-high stone partition separated the two sections against which the hearth was placed, and this, in turn, was eventually discarded and replaced by a chimney either in this partition or in one of the side walls.

The beds in some shielings, especially those on the Ness pastures, were built wholly or partially in the end wall, the wall being made about 9 ft. thick, to accommodate them. Later improvements were the clay plastering and whitewashing of the living quarters and the papering of improvised roofs above the bed. Some of the recesses were also enlarged to hold cupboards. Some of these Spring Houses could be anything from 30 to 50 ft. in length.

Small bothies, called *cotain*, were often built near shielings to house young calves, and so prevent them from suckling their mothers.

These buildings merged completely into the land-scape as it was the heather side of the turf slabs which was uppermost, and although outwardly they looked very primitive, they were warm and cosy inside, and kept scrupulously clean, for each milkmaid, *banachag*, prided herself on the neatness and tidiness of her home and on the hospitality she was able to give her visitors.

The village constables decided the date on which all stock had to be removed beyond the Black Dykes. This was known as *Glanadh a' Bhaile*, Cleansing the Village. This was done usually in the first week in May or whenever the corn was ready to sprout. Preparations for going to the shieling pastures had to be done beforehand. The men went out to repair the ravages of the winter storms and to make the shielings habitable, for it was the custom in many districts, in order to preserve the roof timber, to remove the roof, wholly or partially, and stack the turf slabs and the timber on the bed platform against the wall, as it was felt that the turf thatch would become so heavy with the winter rains that the roofs would collapse. About this time too, if the weather was good, the old cows began to get restless, and instead of returning homewards from the inbye pastures of an evening they led their followers to their summer quarters or *gearraidhean* from where they had to be fetched unwillingly, by irate herds.

When the actual migration day arrived, all the villagers were early astir. There was so much to be done. Chaos seemed to reign, but it was orderly chaos. People shouted, children screeched, dogs barked, cattle lowed, sheep bleated, but in a compara-tively short time a start was made for the distant moors. Even the animals knew what was afoot and seemed as excited as their accompanying humans. Once loosened from their stalls they took to the moor track, needing no driving. The leaders led the cavalcade of animals and humans very purposefully, and seldom stopped even to nibble a mouthful of grass. Calves let loose for the first time in their young lives seemed to go mad. They ran hither and yon, to the danger of breaking bones or of dislocating limbs, with their tails high in the air. It was practically impossible to catch them, or hold them if caught, unless their owners had the foresight to tie rope collars (*braighdein*) around them. The calves soon tired with their new-found freedom and came to seek the protection of their mothers. Some of these youngsters refused to cross the first streams they met with, and yet they would before the end of the summer, unhesitantly, swim across a loch with their heads close to their mothers' flanks.

Only in two districts, Uig and Point, were the shielings distant. The people of Bernera on Uig had to swim their cattle across Bernera Sound (now bridged), before their long trek to their summer dwellings, while the people of Point had, in some cases, to drive their cattle to their shielings by the Lochs Road, beyond Stornoway. In their case, carts were used to carry their goods and chattels. Elsewhere, where only moorland tracks denoted the way to the various shielings, every person going on this migration had to carry a load with all the necessities for a moorland sojourn, for there was no food, or anything else for the benefit of humans, to be found among the heather. Pots, pans, pails, jugs, basins, teapots, crockery, foodstuffs, bedding, extra clothes, ropes (for bogged animals), spades, etc., etc., – all had to be carried, and cheerfully carried, in creels in sacks or in rope-tied bundles.

Inevitably the younger members of both sexes gravitated towards one another, and many a lad arrived at his destination more burdened than when he left his home. This was one of the happiest days in the crofters' calendar: a day full of hope: a day that reminded them of similar days in their youth. The cold dark days of winter lay behind them and ahead were the lonely, lovely brown moors, with their rushing streams and sparkling lochs. Shieling days were days of joy. Seldom did a death occur to mar the pleasure of the stay. When it did the dwelling was seldom or never occupied again. Shieling time was holiday time – not a time for regrets or despair.

Once the cavalcade was well on its way, the herds left their charges to their own devices. They knew that they were no longer needed, so they set off to the shielings on their own, and it gave their burdened followers quite a thrill when they saw smoke arising from the various shielings. The sight seemed to make them lengthen their stride and lighten their burden. Shieling smoke, *Ceò na h-airigh*, seemed always to be different from the peat smoke at home. It was bluer, lighter, and alluring. Once the shieling was reached the various bundles were dumped on the green sward which surrounded each shieling, and while the womenfolk prepared a meal, the youngsters gathered heather tips, rushes, reeds and moorland grasses, for use as bedding, while the menfolk lit as many fires as possible on the bed platforms and on the floors to drive out the winter cold, and any other task which

needed attention. The youngsters made quite certain they were within call when the alfresco meal was ready. After a fervent grace eager hands were quickly stretched for the plain but wholesome fare. Once the fires inside died down and the ashes were removed, the varied articles were placed in their appropriate places. The still warm bed platform was covered with thin, dry turf from the previous year's thatch, then heather was laid on this, followed by rushes or reeds and moorland grass, to form a springy comfortable mattress of which nobody could complain. The bedclothes were arranged in order on this with a blanket between the grass and the lower sheet.

Once everyone was satisfied that everybody was shipshape, the helpers set off for their homes, the men with the prospect of sailing shortly to the East Coast fishing ports, and only the milkmaids, young and old, were left to look after the stock. They only had the cows to look after, for the sheep had their own shepherds, and only in Uig and parts of Ness were horses taken to the shielings after their shoes had been removed. After the cows were milked and the milk set in basins, supper was eaten, and before going to bed a chapter of the Bible was read. A couple of verses were sung and prayers offered up by the mother as she sat by the fireside, with a clean towel covering her hair to show her respect for the Almighty.

No sooner were tired heads and weary bodies between the clean-smelling sheets than the scent of the heather and the pure, strong moorland air seemed to make all powerless. The youngsters were the first to succumb to sleep, but the mother, lying at the front of the bed, brooded over her family for a while. The first night out on the moors was always strange. The wind had a different sound from what it had in the village, and seemed intent on exploring every nook and cranny about the shieling in an attempt to enter. There was a coldness too, for it took at least three days before the stubborn winter cold was expelled from the dwelling. The other shielings seemed far distant. The smoored fire and her sleeping brood were the only familiar things. The odd burst of flame from the smoored fire occasionally disturbed the darkness. Round the bothy she could hear the animal noises which gave her a sense of security. The silence was also occasionally disturbed by the cackling of grouse, the bleating of sheep, the splash of jumping trout. The plaintive cry of curlew or the drumming of the snipe all added to her loneliness, and yet she was content. Soon her eyes too closed, and she slept as safely in her moorland cot, with its unlocked door, as she would with a guard outside. All too soon singing linnets and the morning sunshine streaming through the smokehole heralded the arrival of a new day. Early rising was always necessary on the shielings, for some of the herds had to attend school, miles away. These went most unwillingly, but hurried back again in the evenings. How these lads and lassies were envied by their less fortunate schoolmates, many of whom managed to get themselves invited to spend an occasional Saturday or Sunday on the *airigh*.

Life on the shielings was a busy one, especially where women went home to the villages in the mornings and returned again in the evenings, carrying provisions for humans and animals. Lewis cows were so spoilt that they would only give milk if they were being fed at the same time. Grass and seaweed were greatly appreciated, though when these failed to materialise an old boot or a piece of wood seemed to be quite palatable. When carrying milk in pails the mouth of these receptacles had a piece of damp sheepskin tied round it. As this skin dried, the tighter it became. Moss was used to pack the pails and jars in the creels to keep the various containers from banging against each other. In the case of distant shielings contact was only made with the homes once a week. This visit was very important, as the visitor brought news back with her as well as a fresh supply of foodstuffs.

The chief purpose of the shieling being to provide butter and cheese for the winter months, and to fatten the cattle, it was natural that these should have precedence over all other activities. The milk was allowed to lie in basins for a couple of days before the cream was skimmed. This operation took place morning and evening, and when a sufficient amount of cream was collected this was put into a churn and turned into butter. The buttermilk was greatly appreciated by the herds and calves and by the milkmaids for baking. A calf's stomach usually hung from a rafter where milk, mixed with salt, and dried, was used as rennet to thicken the milk if necessary. This thick milk was placed in a pot over a slow fire and brought to a certain temperature, not unlike that of a baby's bath. It was never allowed to boil or the curds would become hard. The white curds, *crowdie*, were then squeezed to drive out the whey and some salt added, and placed in a wooden vat called a *fiodhan*

where they were left under pressure until they became cheese, which was then hung from a rope to finish the drying properly. The whey was as greatly appreciated as the buttermilk.

The cows also had to be carefully herded, for there are plenty of bogs on the Lewis moors and the cows knew the best grasses grew in such marshes. It was interesting to see these animals crossing wet ground. It looked as if they had an inbuilt sonar system of their own to test the depth of the peat, snorting as they went. They could also cross daintily from rush-tuft to rush-tuft in a marsh. Bogging was quite frequent, though. This was why ropes were necessary to help drag them to safety. When this was being done it was necessary first to bend the forelegs and put firm turf under them. This gave the stranded cow the necessary foundation from which to try and extricate herself.

Peats had also to be cut, dried and stacked for the following year. Particular care was taken to keep the shielings as clean and cosy as possible. The bed-clothes and the bedding were carried outside to be aired fairly frequently. Every day the bed-clothes were folded carefully and placed at the head of the bed and kept covered with a cover, *cuibhrig*.

Life on the shielings for children was as idyllic as life could possibly be, especially at weekends and at holiday times. Herding could be quite pleasant, as other activities could be engaged in at the same time such as swimming, trout-fishing and bird nesting. There was always plenty to eat too – butter, buttermilk, cream, crowdie, cheese, whey, blackberries, crowberries, trout, and in early summer, eggs. Perhaps the less said about eggs, the better, as many birds are protected by law, and the Lewis proprietors at one time appointed old soldiers to patrol the moors at shieling time to curb the youthful predators. These old men were called *Bodaich nan Cearcan Fraoich*, Old Grouse Men. Plovers, ducks, grouse, herons, sea-gulls, geese and the black-throated diver all supplied their quota. The eggs of plovers, ducks and grouse were excellent; the others had a rather fishy taste. To test the freshness or otherwise of the eggs, they were placed in a shallow pool. If they lay flat they were fresh, but if the rounded end rose ever so slightly, then they were not, and these eggs were returned to where they came from. No nest was ever wholly cleared.

The summer months passed all too quickly, for there

was plenty of entertainment on the shielings. Evening ceilidhs were frequent. Visitors from other shielings were welcome. The pipes and melodeons were often heard by lonely lochs, but all good things have to end, and when the last evening on the shielings came, usually the last Friday in July, there was a mixture of sadness and happiness: very mixed feelings. This night was called *Oidhche na h-Iomraich*, the Night of the Flitting. There was little or no sleep for anyone that night, except for the very young, for many people had come to help to carry things home. Everything which could be eaten was eaten. Dancing and singing went on all night.

After breakfast, if such it could be called, packing was begun. When everything portable was ready, then the bedding was taken out and set on fire. This was a signal to the cows that it was time to turn their backs on the moors and make for their homes, and they headed for the villages as willingly as they had left them three months earlier, but they were in a way completely different animals, sleek, frisky, semi-wild; totally different from the skinny specimens they had been then. They carried themselves differently too.

It was with a feeling of sadness that people always left the shielings. The shortening days and the awareness of the passing years was on them all. Each wondered if ever they would revisit these hallowed haunts of childhoold, or what changes life would bring before they returned, if they ever did return, the following year. Many of those who took part in this night in 1914 found graves in France, Flanders, Egypt and the Oceans of the World. The First World War ended shieling life, although it struggled on in odd places for some years.

Now the moors are desolate. Lochs and glens never hear the sound of happy laughter. The curlew and the plaintive snipe scurry across in the twilight, but no child snuggles closer to his mother as their eerie cries are heard. Nothing is left to these shielings but green mounds, rickles of stones and a few odd stones upended where cows used to rub themselves.

Here is where R. L. Stevenson's poem, 'Exiles', is really understood:

> Grey recumbent tombs of the dead in desert places;
> Standing stones on the vacant wine-red moors;
> Hills of sheep, and the howes of the silent vanished races
> And winds austere and pure.

The Clay Tobacco Pipe Collection in the National Museum

A Sharp

Although the collection of clay tobacco pipes in the National Museum of Antiquities of Scotland is much smaller than that in many English museums, it is nevertheless comparable in size with the collections in most Scottish museums. There are over three hundred pipes, with examples from Scotland, England, Holland and a very few from Ireland. The majority are Scottish, and are of seventeenth century origin, but there are several fascinating exceptions. Strangely, there are relatively few later pipes from the nineteenth and twentieth centuries. One would normally expect these more numerous and recently made pipes to form the major part of the collection. Probably the museum has few later pipes because they were so common that the casual finder saw no real merit in them. In any case, the documentary evidence relating to later makers is adequate. Nevertheless, all those bearing makers' marks are of value in that all evidence, particularly regarding the sale of pipe moulds to other manufacturers, must be sifted and examined to produce a clear picture of the state of the Scottish industry. Of particular interest are the short-term makers, who worked for only a year or two before going out of business. A short, illustrated list of later makers in Scotland is appended.

The early pipes constitute the most interesting part of the collection. They date from the earliest years of the seventeenth century to the early years of the eighteenth, leaving a considerable chronological gap in the later sequence. Such a gap is found often in collections, and in archaeological groups. A possible explanation lies in the increased taking of snuff in this period. The American revolution from 1776 onwards may also have played a part, for as the Glasgow tobacco importers hoarded their stocks, and the price of tobacco rose, so would sales have fallen, and demand for pipes have lessened. This, however, would have been contributory only, not causal.

That the pipe-making industry was extant in Scotland by 1622 at least is demonstrated by both documentary evidence and by an examination of the shapes of the pipe bowls. On the documentary side, we have the information that 'Thomas Deyne deponis to William Hutton that at sindrie tymes he hes boght fra William Bankis, tobacco pype maker in the Canogait, ten pund weight [of tobacco] or thairby, quhair of the said Bankis pay it the custome'.[1]

William Banks, who died in January 1659, was probably the leading pipemaker in Edinburgh throughout this period. His pipes, although far from uniform in shape (a fact which denotes the rapidity of change in fashionable shapes), all carry the relief initials 'W.B.' on the sides of the heel at the base of the bowl. Generally, the 'W' is on the left side of the bowl, as seen by the smoker, and the 'B' is on the right side. Occasionally, the letters are reversed, probably by accident. There is no evidence of a maker with the initials 'B.W.' at this time. Some of Banks' pipes carry an impressed stamp of a three-towered castle on the base of the bowl. This points to Edinburgh manufacture, much like the similar mark used by silversmiths. It appears that Banks had held a monopoly from the Crown in the manufacture of clay pipes, for a complaint in 1642 stated that the bailies of the Canongate and the Provost and bailies of Edinburgh could not assist Mr Banks in seeking out pipes made by others in the kingdom, as all monopolies pertaining to tobacco had been declared ineffectual by the late Parliament. From this document[2] we can deduce that Banks had held a monopoly, and we can also see that it was breached by unofficial manufacturers. One person in particular is mentioned, a Richard Calder, identified as the manager of an Edinburgh pipe works. Banks had caused the factory to be raided, and a large number of Calder's pipes to be destroyed. Thus we have undeniable evidence that Banks held neither a legal nor a *de facto* monopoly in pipemaking in 1642. The museum holds nineteen of William Banks' pipes.

There are numerous examples of pipes which are typologically contemporaneous with those of Banks, and some seem to predate his work. We must now try to establish the criteria for differentiating bowl types chronologically, though a definitive typology is not at present feasible. In fact the variety of bowl forms from the early period is so wide that it is hard to say much regarding a possible sequence of the early pipes. We can ascribe to them an early date, but no real and definitive order can be achieved. The first and major criterion is the size of the bowl itself. In the early period bowls were small, but grew in size as the industry progressed. The growth can be ascribed to the increasing availability, and progressive cheapness, of tobacco. A second equally important criterion is the development in bowl shape. Early bowls (nos. 1-3) have quite straight, non-bulbous sides. Numbers 1 and 3 in particular have curiously crude 'planar' sides, as though a very crude mould had been used. There is no evidence on them of a 'chin', that is a scalloped curve above the foot of the bowl at the front. Neither they, nor number 2, which is a remarkable and very singular pipe, have any markings on them. Makers' numbers are of great use in dating pipes, and in determining their place of origin. With the exception of the pipes of William Banks, few early pipes carry marks. Numbers 4-6 are exceptions. All three carry basal castle stamps, implying Edinburgh manufacture. These are unlikely to be later in date than 1630, and are probably ten years earlier. These early pipes bear a similarity, in some cases, to a dated group (c. 1600-1637) found in Edinburgh High Street.[3] The slight increase in bulbousness of the front wall of the pipes should be noted, as this marks a definite trend. There is also a pronounced forward rake of the bowl, and a slightly increased chin above the heel. The next six bowls display both dimensional growth and the development of a rounded bowl form. The sequence, at its end, has also started to develop a definite chin. The development of this feature continues[6] until the late years of the seventeenth century. It is at this point that we can look at some examples of William Banks' work. The pipes numbered 14-16 are all by Banks, and the bulbous bowl, and the development of the chin, can be seen clearly. The workmanship is quite crude, particularly when compared with number 12, which was a polished, and probably quite expensive, pipe. The

three Banks' pipes were probably made more for the mass market, in all likelihood, between 1630 and 1650. Number 15 carries a basal castle stamp.

William Banks had a son, John, who also became involved in pipemaking. The museum has several examples of John's produce, which again carries relief initials on the bowl sides. John was certainly working by 1659, when he became Burgess of the Canongate.[4] There are some pipes with the relief initials 'T.B.' These may have been the work of one Thomas Banks, who, according to the Register of Deeds, was a manufacturer in Leith in 1661. Whether Thomas was related to William and John is not known, but there is one pipe in the museum's collection which does not carry the heel-side relief initials, but an impressed basal stamp. This three-letter stamp has the initials 'T.B.' above the letter 'L'. This appears to confirm Thomas as the maker, the letter 'L' signifying 'Leith' (No. 18). It should be noted that English three-letter marks carry the initial of the town of origin above those of the maker, whereas in Scotland the makers' initials surmount that of the town of origin. Number 17 may be an example of Thomas Banks' work, similar in shape and size to William Banks' bowls.

However, the difference in bowl shape between numbers 17 and 18 is obvious. At the period in question, between 1660 and 1670, a domestic change in the shape of bowls is evident. They became taller, with far more graceful lines, and a most pronounced 'overhang' at the front of the bowl. In addition, the 'chin' is fully developed, and the foot of the bowl becomes slightly splayed. A pipe by Patrick Crawford of Edinburgh, which has a three-lettered basal stamp, illustrates this (No. 19). This bowl shape now appears to become the norm, and part of a more unified trend in bowl shape development, as can be seen in numbers 20 to 25. Two of these bowls (Nos. 20 and 21) have three-letter basal marks. These have the initial 'I.C.' above a letter 'G'. This may be the mark of James Colquhon, a Glasgow manufacturer and Burgess in 1668.[5] There are also pipes carrying the relief initials 'I.C.' on the sides of the heel. It may well be that these are down-market pipes by the same maker. The similarity in bowl shapes is very strong, however, and they are probably by Colquhon.

The five pipes from 26 to 30 inclusive demonstrate the continued trend to around 1730. It is at this point that the Scottish pipes start to decrease in numbers. Three of these pipes have basal castle stamps. One has the relief initials of Patrick Crawford, whose wife carried on his business after his death. The manufacturer with the initials 'W.I.' is unknown, but number 29 is by John Aiken, who worked in Glasgow around 1700. The larger bowl shapes, with flatter sides, can be seen clearly in this sequence.

Thus, by 1730, there is an established move to uniformity in bowl size and shape, relative to the rather chaotic variety of shapes in the early years of the seventeenth century. Further, larger-scale manufacturers appear to be establishing themselves from the mid-century onwards, possibly at the expense of the smaller traders.

The collection contains a number of Dutch pipes, of which roughly half carry the relief 'Tudor rose' form of decoration on the bowl sides. The mark comprises seven or eight raised dots (one centrally placed, and the others surrounding it). Some of these have stamens between the dots, which in turn represent the petals of the flower. One bowl carries a relief fleur-de-lis on each side of the bowl, and there are two 'Raleigh' pipes in the collection. These feature the moulded head of Sir Walter Raleigh facing the smoker, apparently being eaten by a crocodile. These pipes appear to be derived from the legend that Sir Walter, whilst on his travels, was swallowed whole by a crocodile, only to be regurgitated by the reptile because his body was impregnated with tobacco. The Dutch pipes (Nos. 31-35) all date from the seventeenth century. Number 35 shows the later trend to spurred pipes. This fine example has a superbly decorated stem, featuring fleurs-de-lis and strip-and-dot decoration.

A slightly larger number of English pipes, mostly from the north-west or London, completes the collection. Most bowls are pre-1690 in date, and are spurred with bulbous bowls. These are from north-west England, and several have hemispherical stamps containing makers' initials on the back of the bowl. They are very similar to those of South Lancashire type[6] (Nos. 36-38). The few London pipes tend to be small, bulbous, and of very early manufacture.

Although the Dutch and English pipes are of interest in themselves, it must be said that the Scottish pipes are of greater importance to the collection, in that they provide at least a starting point for a future Scottish typology. Of particular interest is the transitional period of 1650-70, where the bowl form underwent such a dramatic development. It is also hoped that, in the future, the confusion surrounding the plethora of early pipes will be resolved satisfactorily.

Acknowledgements:

I would like to record my thanks to the National Museum of Antiquities of Scotland for allowing me access to its collection; Dr. David Caldwell, whose good advice and encouragement have been invaluable; and Peter Davey of the Institute of Extension Studies in Liverpool for his advice regarding bowl typology.

Pre-1730 Scottish pipemakers whose work is represented in the Museum's collection.

Particular marks	Full name	Place	Date	Source
	John Agnew	Glasgow	1849-57	
A.A.	Alex^r· Aikine	Glasgow	1/10/1722	G:B.R 1537-70
A.A.	Andrew Aikine	Glasgow	1/10/1722	G:B.R 1537-70
I.A.	John Aikine son of John A. below	Glasgow		
I.A.	John Aikine		2/5/1700	GBR 1537-70
I.B.	John Banks	Edinburgh	2/9/1659	C.B.R.
T.B.	Thos. Banks	Edinburgh	1/4/1670	Reg. of Deeds
W.B.	Wm. Banks	Edinburgh	3/9/1629	C.B.R.
			25/1/1659	C.R.M.
T.B.	T. Barwick	Edinburgh	c. 1660	1975 BAR
S.B.	Stephen Bell	Edinburgh	c. 1649	
I.C.	James Colquhon	Glasgow	c. 1668	J. A. Fleming: *Scottish Pottery*
P.C.	Patrick Crawford	Edinburgh		
S.H.	Samuel Hyenshaw		1747	1974 BAR
W.Y.	Walter Young	Edinburgh	1690	E.MR.
W.Y.	William Young	Edinburgh	1667	E.MR.

19th and 20th century pipemakers whose work is represented in the Museum's collection.

John Agnew	Glasgow	1849-57
J. & G. Burton	Cupar	
John Christie	Glasgow	1863-70
Wm. Christie	Glasgow	1857-1962
	Edinburgh	1894-1962
Alexander Coghill	Glasgow	1826-1904
Duncan	Dundee	
J. Gray	Balmullo	
A. Kane	Dundee	1874-93
John Miller	Glasgow	1866-8
Duncan McDougall & Co.	Glasgow	1847-1968
J. McKenzie	Edinburgh	1864-83
J. Scroggie	Glasgow	1873-86
William Swaney	Edinburgh	1881
T. Whyte & Co.	Edinburgh	1832-64
Wm. Whyte & Sons	Glasgow	1805-1955
William C. Wood	Glasgow	1857-75

The dates pertaining to these makers were found in the 1975 British Archaeological Reports, edited by Adrian Oswald.

Notes

1. *Register of the Privy Council of Scotland (RPC)* XIV 588
2. *RPC* Vol VII 2nd series 324-5
3. *Proceedings of the Society of Antiquaries of Scotland* 106 (1975-6) 218
4. Scottish Record Society (SRS) Canongate Burgess Roll
5. SRS Glasgow Burgess Roll
6. *British Archaeological Reports* (BAR) 78, 1980. Clay Pipes III 131

Abbreviations

C.B.R. — Canongate Burgess Roll
C.R.M. — Canongate Register of Marriages
E.R.M. — Edinburgh Marriage Roll
G.B.R. — Glasgow Burgess Roll

A brief description of the illustrated pipes (scale: pipes, 1:1; stamps, 2:1)

1. A very small clay tobacco pipe bowl, possibly hand made. It has a very small heel, but no marks.
    Fabric — very hard, with many inclusions of a granite nature.
    Stem bore — $\frac{9}{64}''$

2. Unmarked bowl of clay pipe. The bowl is small, with a wide mouth, and possibly crude rouletting or scalloping at the rim.
    The fabric is soft, with few inclusions.
    Stem bore — $\frac{1}{8}''$

3. Scottish clay tobacco pipe bowl, c. 1620. Small capacity, with milled rim. Unmarked. It has a pedestal heel, and a definite forward rake to the bowl.
    Fabric is soft, white, with mica inclusions.
    Stem bore — $\frac{1}{8}''$

4. Bowl of Scottish pipe, c. 1610-30. Small and bulbous, with milling at the slightly narrower rim. The heel is small and flat, with a basal castle stamp.
    Fabric is quite hard — many medium-sized mica inclusions.

5. Scottish pipe bowl, c. 1610-30, bulbous with a pedestal heel, which carries an impressed basal castle stamp. Milling (crude) on bowl rim.
    Fabric — soft with few inclusions.
    Stem bore — $\frac{1}{8}''$

6. Pipe bowl — slender, only slightly bulbous with rough rouletting near the rim. The heel is slightly chinned, with a basal castle stamp, signifying Edinburgh manufacture.
    Probably c. 1610-30
    Fabric — soft, white, very pure.
    Stem bore — $\frac{1}{8}''$

7. Clay pipe bowl, with rouletting at rim. Bowl has forward tilt, slight chin, and a flat heel which joins the stem. No marks.
    c. 1620-30
    Fabric — soft with small inclusions.
    Stem bore — $\frac{7}{64}''$

8. Bowl of clay pipe — virtually no chin, but pronounced forward tilt. Bowl is quite bulbous and carries crude incuse cross on the back. Traces of rouletting at the rim. No marks.
    Probably c. 1620-40
    Fabric — very hard and full of large inclusions.
    Stem bore — $\frac{3}{32}''$

9. Bowl of clay pipe, bulbous with no chin and some rouletting. Flat heel, at same level as stem. No marks.
    c. 1640
    Fabric is soft and white.
    Stem bore — $\frac{7}{64}''$

10. Clay pipe bowl, with bulbous bowl, and deeply rouletted rim. Heel joins stem. Some chinning. No marks.
    c. 1640
    Fabric — soft. white, fine.
    Stem bore — $\frac{1}{8}''$

11. Bowl and part of stem of clay pipe. It has a bulbous bowl with crude rouletting at the rim. It has a slight chin, with a flat, pedestal heel.
    Probably c. 1630-1660
    Fabric — soft with large inclusions.
    Stem bore — $\frac{3}{32}''$

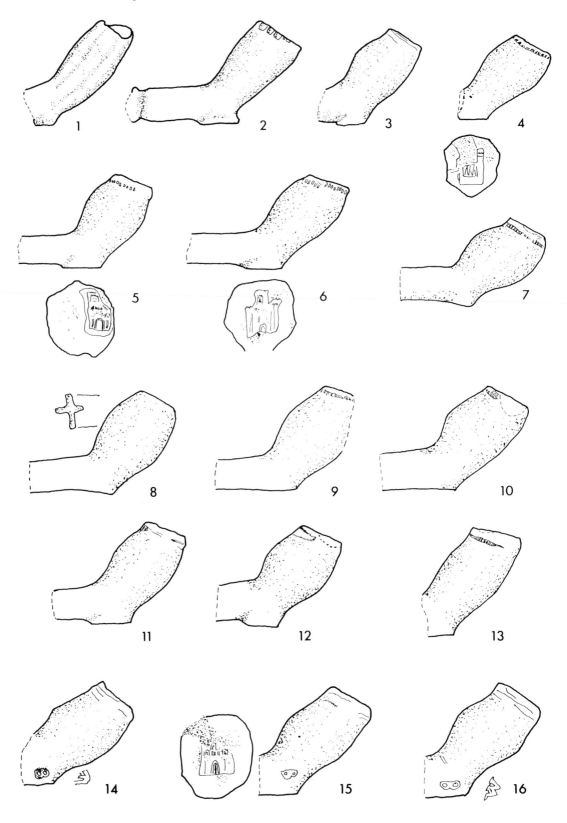

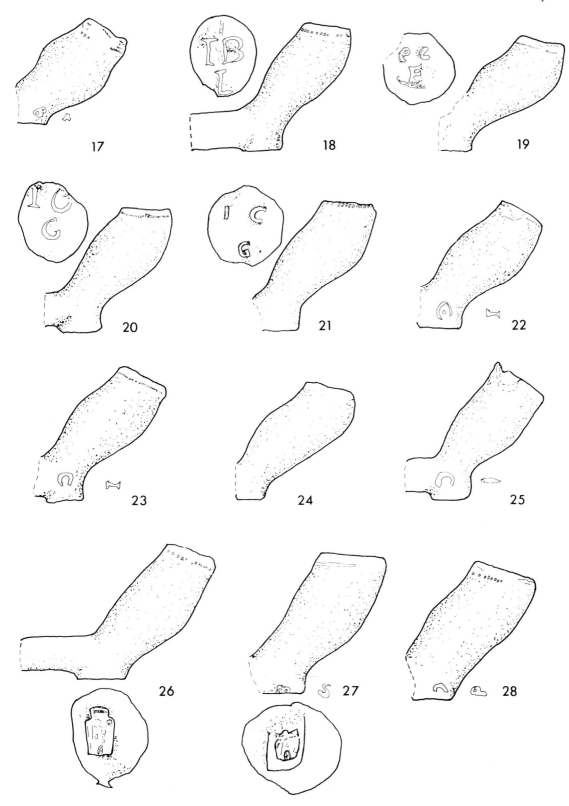

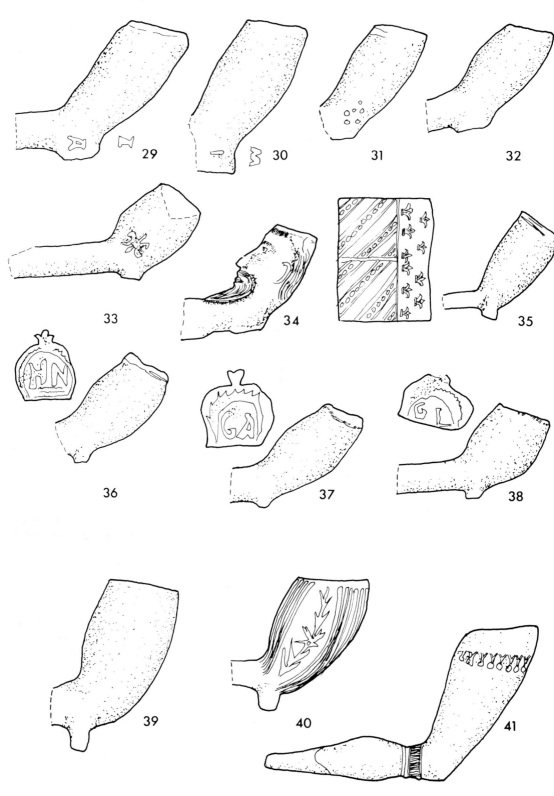

29

30

31

32

33

34

35

36

37

38

39

40

41

12. Bowl and part of stem of clay pipe. The bowl and heel are tilted forward, the bowl being slightly bulbous with rouletting at the rim. The heel is slightly chinned, but is unmarked. The pipe may have been polished.

    Probably c. 1640-60

    Fabric – very hard.
    Stem bore – $\frac{7}{64}''$

13. Clay pipe bowl – straight sided with some chinning. Offset rouletting at rim. Wide mouth to bowl. Heel is wide, round and unmarked.

    c. 1640

    Fabric – quite soft with some micaceous inclusions.
    Stem bore – $\frac{7}{64}''$

14. Bowl of clay pipe – it has quite bulbous sides, and fine deep rouletting below the rim. The chinned heel carries relief initials 'W.B.' on its sides. Maker – Wm. Banks, of Edinburgh.

    Probably c. 1640-60

    Fabric – hard, with many inclusions.
    Stem bore – $\frac{1}{8}''$

15. Bowl of clay tobacco pipe, unused, with crude rouletting at the rim. It has slightly bulbous sides. The heel sides carry the relief initials 'W.B.' A basal castle stamp confirms Edinburgh as the place of manufacture.

    c. 1640-60

    Fabric – hard, coarse.
    Stem bore – $\frac{4}{64}''$

16. Bowl of clay pipe, bulbous with rouletted rim. It has the relief initials 'W.B.' on the heel sides. Some chinning to the bowl.

    c. 1640-60

    Fabric – soft, white, with some large inclusions.
    Stem bore – $\frac{3}{32}''$

17. Bowl of clay pipe – longer than the above, but still slightly bulbous. Rough rouletting at the lip. Heel is chinned slightly, and carries relief initials 'T.B.' on its sides.

    c. 1640-60

    Fabric – quite soft, but with many inclusions and mica traces.
    Stem bore – $\frac{1}{8}''$

18. Clay pipe bowl with rough rouletting near the rim. Basal initials 'T.B.', above 'L'. Very deep, chinned heel, with little splaying. Bowl is long, with frontal overhang.

    c. 1650-70

    Fabric – quite hard, with medium inclusions.
    Stem bore – $\frac{1}{8}''$

19. Bowl of clay pipe, with very deep, chinned heel and fine rouletting at the rim. The base has incuse initials 'P.C.' above 'E'. Maker is probably Patrick Crawford, of Edinburgh.

    c. 1650-70

Fabric – very fine with small inclusions.
Stem bore – $\frac{7}{64}''$

20. Pipe bowl with deep chin and slightly splayed heel. Fine rouletting at rim. Heel has basal initials 'I.C.' and 'G'. Probably by James Colquhon of Glasgow.

    c. 1660-80

    Fabric – white, soft with fine inclusions.
    Stem bore – $\frac{7}{64}''$

21. Bowl of clay pipe – with deeply chinned heel and frontal overhang to bowl. Fine rouletting at rim. The heel is deep, splayed and chinned, with the basal initials 'I.C.' above 'G'.

    c. 1660-80

    Fabric – quite hard with some inclusions.
    Stem bore – $\frac{1}{8}''$

22. Bowl of clay pipe – with deeply chinned heel. Has letters 'I.C.' mould in relief on sides of the heel. Rouletted near the rim.

    c. 1660-80

    Fabric – hard with many inclusions.
    Stem bore – $\frac{1}{8}''$

23. As 22, but with soft, granular fabric.

    c. 1660-80

    Stem bore – $\frac{7}{64}''$

24. Bowl of clay pipe, with deeply chinned small heel.

    c. 1670

    Fabric – soft, with medium sized inclusions.
    No stem bore measurements.

25. Bowl of clay pipe – deeply chinned heel. No rouletting. It carries the letters 'T.C.' in relief on the heel sides. Maker not known.

    c. 1670-90

    Fabric – soft with large inclusions
    Stem bore – $\frac{1}{8}''$

26. Bowl of clay pipe with rough rouletting at the rim. The bowl bulges in the middle, and narrows towards the base, giving an overhang effect. The heel is large, pedestal, and flat, with a basal castle stamp.

    c. 1670-90

    Fabric – quite soft with large inclusions.
    Stem bore – $\frac{3}{32}''$

27. Bowl of clay pipe, with wide mouth and bulged front. Rough rouletting below the rim. The deep heel carries the relief initials 'S.B.' on its sides. Incuse basal castle stamp.

    c. 1680-1720

    Fabric – soft with many inclusions.
    Stem bore – $\frac{1}{8}''$

28. Wide-mouthed long pipe bowl with crude rouletting below the rim. Heel sides carry relief initials 'P.C.' Probably by Patrick Crawford of Edinburgh, or his wife.

    c. 1680-1700

D

Fabric — soft with small inclusions.
No stem bore measurement.

29. Bowl and part of stem of clay pipe. No rouletting. Wide mouth, straight sides. Deep heel, with bowl tapering towards it. Heel sides carry relief initials 'I.A' Probably by John Aikine of Glasgow.

c. 1700

Fabric — soft with small to moderate inclusions.
Stem bore — $\frac{1}{8}''$

30. Bowl of clay pipe, long with straight sides, and fine rouletting at the rim. The heel is chinned and has a basal castle stamp. Relief initials 'W.I.' on sides of heel (maker unknown).
Fabric — hard with many inclusions.
No stem bore measurement.

31. Bowl of Dutch clay pipe, with very small heel, slightly chinned. Straight sided bowl, with fine rouletting. Relief 'Tudor Rose' motif on bowl sides.

c. 1680

Fabric — soft with mica flakes.
No stem bore measurement.

32. Plain, slender clay pipe bowl of Dutch origin. Forward tilted, the bowl has rouletting on the rim. The heel is chinned and pedestal, and is unmarked.

c. 1620

Fabric is very soft and white, with few inclusions.
Stem bore — $\frac{7}{64}''$

33. Bowl and part of stem of Dutch clay pipe, with relief fleur-de-lis on both sides. Rouletting at rim. Bulbous bowl and small heel suggest pre-1650 date.
Fabric — soft fine, with small inclusions.
Stem bore $\frac{1}{8}''$

34. Bowl of a Dutch 'Raleigh' pipe of the late 17th century. Of slightly crude workmanship with rouletting visible at bowl top. Heel is small, circular.
Fabric — very soft, fine.
Stem bore — $\frac{3}{32}''$

35. Small Dutch bowl, c. 1700, with fine rouletting at rim, and very finely moulded stem. Polished.
Fabric — hard with few inclusions.
Stem bore — $\frac{3}{32}''$

36. Bowl of North-Western English spurred pipe, c. 1660-80. Fine rouletting at rim. Bowl is spurred, forward leaning, and bulbous, with a stamped decorated semi-circle on the bowl back enclosing the letters H.N.
Fabric — soft with few inclusions.
Stem bore — $\frac{7}{64}''$

37. As 36, but with initials 'G.A.'

38. As 36, but with initials 'G.L.'

39. Bowl of spurred pipe, c. 1820-70. Upright, slightly bulged bowl of very large size.
Fabric — soft, brittle with few inclusions.
Stem bore — $\frac{3}{32}''$

40. Bowl of 19th century pipe, with fluted decoration on all sides, and a relief tobacco plant motif on either side. Large, heavy spur.
Fabric — soft with few inclusions.
Stem bore — $\frac{3}{32}''$

41. Novelty clay pipe in shape of gartered woman's leg. Late 19th century.
Fabric — quite soft with many small inclusions.
Stem bore — $\frac{3}{32}''$

Wet-Nursing in Scotland: 1500-1800

Rosalind K Marshall

On 13th November, 1618, the Dowager Countess of Winton, always ready to give her family helpful advice, sent a letter to her daughter-in-law Anna, Countess of Eglinton. Usually her missives were somewhat critical in tone, but this time she was approving. 'As concerning your daughter Elinor,' she wrote, 'I am very glaid that ye have gottin ane young milk woman to hir, seing hir Mamye proved not sufficient. Ye have done verye wyselie in doing the samyn, for the young milk, with the help of God, will bring hir to again'.[1]

This solution to the problem of a baby who was not thriving may seem strange to the modern reader, but wet-nursing had been an established practice even in Biblical times. By the eleventh century, it appears to have been fairly common through Western Europe, and in the sixteenth century it was an accepted mode of procedure for wealthy families in both Scotland and England. Mary of Guise is known to have employed a wet-nurse for her children, and when James VI made his first appearance before the English ambassador, it was in the arms of his wet-nurse.[2]

1. *Anne Hay, Countess of Winton,* 1625, by Adam de Colone. (In the Collection of the Scottish National Portrait Gallery).

2. *Mary of Guise,* by Corneille de Lyon. (In the Collection of the Scottish National Portrait Gallery).

Not only do we have documentary knowledge of the conventional kind, but it is interesting to note that in ballads and traditional tales, the mortal woman pressed into service to suckle the child of a fairy was almost a stock character in Scotland as well as in

Germany and Scandinavia. One popular Nithsdale story told of a young mother confronted by a woman in a fairy mantle, carrying an infant swaddled in green silk. She was asked to nurse the child and, when she had done so successfully, was rewarded with a trip to fairyland. Another highly popular ballad, 'The Queen of Elfland's Nourice', told how a mortal mother was carried off to serve as wet-nurse in the elf-queen's family and was released only when the child was old enough to walk.[3]

Despite the fact that the wet-nurse was an accepted figure in society, her role was not untouched by controversy, for breast-feeding by the natural mother remained the ideal. Throughout the Middle Ages the Virgo Lactans was a particularly popular image, and early medical writers always stressed that the mother's own milk was best.[4] Even at that early period the part played by breast-feeding in the forming of the emotional bond between mother and child was recognised, and it was agreed that a more rewarding maternal relationship was established when the mother did suckle her own baby.[5]

More important even than that, however, were the properties of the milk itself. So highly valued were its nutritional qualities that at least until the early eighteenth century in Scotland human milk was considered to be a singularly effective tonic for adults and children alike. Blind Harry the poet, writing in the 1470s, described an incident when his hero William Wallace, having been rescued from the English in a poor physical state, was tended by his own fostermother. She had a daughter with a twelve-week-old son, and this young woman 'her childis pape in Wallace mouth scho gaiff', with the happy effect that 'the womannys mylk recomford him full swyth' and he was soon restored to health.[6]

Nor was this merely a figment of the literary imagination. Seventeenth-century correspondence provides further evidence. In 1685, for example, Lady Katherine Murray was telling her sister, 'I have so much milk that I give my lord and my son sometimes a drink, for I'm forsed to milk my breasts'. Archibald Pitcairn, the celebrated Edinburgh doctor, was in 1701 advising one of his patients to take 'ane ass-milk diet, or a woman's, by sucking', and almost thirty years later Sir George Steuart of Grandtully's brother was pleased to hear that 'Lady Steuart takes woman's milck . . . I'm convinced it's the best thing could have been advised for her'.[7]

3. *Katherine Hamilton, Duchess of Atholl, formerly Lady Katherine Murray*, by an unknown artist. (In the Collection of the Duke of Atholl).

Important as its nutritional qualities were, milk had other properties which gave it an almost magical significance in the minds of sixteenth- and seventeenth-century men and women. Anatomical knowledge being sadly incomplete, even the medical authorities themselves were convinced that the mother's milk was actually her menstrual blood which was suppressed for the nine months of pregnancy to feed the child in the womb, then was diverted to the breasts, there to be transformed into the more visually acceptable white, frothy milk. This curious notion had important implications which were to underlie all thinking about wet-nursing at least until the end of the seventeenth century. Because nourishment both before and after birth was believed to come directly from the mother's blood, it was regarded as being highly inadvisable to interrupt the natural sequence by 'changing bloods' and introducing a wet-nurse. It also followed that physical and temperamental traits were transferred to the child, not only *in utero* but after birth too, from the milk of whoever suckled him. This belief was succinctly put by Dr. Hugh Chamberlen in his popular translation of a French medical treatise. 'As the nurse is, so will the child be,' he explained, 'by means of the nourishment which it draweth from her, and in sucking her it will draw in both the vices of her body and mind'.[8]

No less a person than James VI himself was a convinced believer in these theories, and on more than one occasion he drew attention to the fact that he had been suckled by a Protestant wet-nurse instead of by his Roman Catholic mother. When urged by the Pope to change his religion, he is said to have replied, 'I suckte Protestante's milk' and later, when he made his opening speech to his first English parliament on 19th March, 1604, he declared, 'I thank God I sucked the milk of God's truth with the milk of my nurse'. These were not merely metaphorical forms of expression, and a year later he was an enthusiastic auditor at a Latin disputation at Oxford on the question, 'Are morals of nurses imbibed by babies with their milk?'[9] His queen obviously shared his views, and according to one account, was most indignant when it was suggested that she should employ a wet-nurse. 'Will I let my child, the child of a king, suck the milk of a subject and mingle the royal blood with the blood of a servant?' she apparently exclaimed.[10]

The transference of qualities from nurse to child was, of course, an overwhelming argument against wet-nursing, yet it seems that in the seventeenth and eighteenth centuries in Scotland, as elsewhere in Western Europe, the practice was becoming increasingly popular. It is always difficult to find evidence, because the nurturing of infants is not a subject which occurs in the usual correspondence of the period. However, here and there, a lady's letter has been preserved in which there is some mention of the subject, and it would seem from these that the reason for employing a wet-nurse was usually a strictly practical one. When the mother died in childbed, for example, there was no other way of ensuring that the baby survived. Certainly, attempts were made from time to time to feed infants with cow's milk from a cow's horn, or from a wooden bottle, or even to force upon them a mixture of bread and milk, or premasticated meat, but such attempts almost invariably had fatal consequences. A wet-nurse was the only answer, and so James Boswell was able to note with satisfaction in his journal of 1780 that by lending out her own wet-nurse to Colonel Mure Campbell, Mrs Boswell had been instrumental in saving the life of the Colonel's motherless daughter.[11]

Likewise, when the mother had endured a difficult confinement, it was often felt that she was not strong enough to breast-feed her own child. Mary Somerville, the celebrated mathematician, was to record that, after her own birth in 1780, her mother was so ill that 'my aunt, who was about to wean her second daughter Janet . . . nursed me till a wet-nurse could be found'.[12] Other mothers, eager to breast-feed, discovered that they did not have enough milk. That had been the Countess of Eglinton's difficulty in 1618, and in like manner the Reverend Alexander Carlyle's wife, 'after trying [in] vain to nurse', gave her second daughter to 'a very faithful and trusty woman in Fisherrow'.[13]

Probably quite a number of mothers were misled by a lack of physiological knowledge. Milk does not actually appear until two or three days after childbirth. The colostrum which precedes it is equally valuable for the baby, whose sucking stimulates lactation, but even in our own time there are mothers who do not realise this, assume that they have little or no milk of their own, and abandon what would have been a successful attempt at breast-feeding. All the modern problems of suckling an infant were magnified in an age when medical knowledge was so lacking, so it is not really surprising that an unusually large number of seventeenth- and eighteenth-century mothers genuinely believed that their milk was insufficient.[14]

As well as apparent inability to breast-feed, there were other reasons why mothers deliberately decided not to make the attempt. Some wives were persuaded by their husbands to hire a wet-nurse because they were anxious to resume marital relations. There had long been a superstitious belief that a mother would spoil her milk if she engaged in sexual intercourse. William Hay, the canon lawyer, mentioned this theory in his lectures on marriage in the sixteenth century, and although he discounted it, he did advise against the resumption of marital relations until the child had been weaned, because of the danger that the wife 'will conceive and that the milk will fall off or be insufficient to feed the child'. On the other hand, since women believed that lactation had a contraceptive effect (a subject still debated today), it is equally likely that there were some wives who were eager to breast-feed rather than embark upon yet another pregnancy.[15]

Writers discussing the subject of infant feeding always claimed that large numbers of women employed wet-nurses because they did not want to interrupt their round of social engagements or spoil their figures by nursing. This charge is difficult to prove or disprove. Obviously those mothers who did hire a wet-nurse out of vanity or laziness were not going to admit to these motives. It is true that by the 1690s Scotswomen knew of recipes 'for puting back the milk in thos that dous not intend tou giv ther chyld the brest', but the number of women who casually abandoned their maternal role should not be exaggerated.[16] At least until the end of the seventeenth century there is no hint that aristocratic Scottish ladies were using wet-nurses as a means of escaping from their domestic responsibilities. Indeed, the overwhelming impression to be gained from their correspondence is that those who did hand their babies over to someone else were almost neurotically anxious about the outcome.

The choice of nurse was, of course, a matter of gravest importance. Even when the notion that personal qualities could be transmitted was finally set aside, there was still the fact that the baby would spend most of his time with the nurse, so that his physical and emotional well-being was her responsibility. Dr. Hugh Chamberlen's readers were accordingly advised to employ a woman who had 'a sweet voice to please and rejoice the child, and likewise she ought to have a clear and free pronunciation that he may not learn an ill accent from her, as usually redhaired nurses have'. Nicholas Culpeper, whose *Directory for Midwives* was published in Edinburgh in 1668, recommended that the nurse be 'of middle stature, fleshy but not fat; of a merry, pleasant, cheerful countenance and ruddy colour, very clear skin that you may see her veins through it'. She must also have a sociable nature, for the ideal nurse 'loves company, cannot endure to be alone; not given to anger but infinitely to playing and singing, she delights much in children and therefore is the fittest nurse for one'.[17]

The somewhat condescending tone of the recommendations arose from the fact that the women who undertook this role were invariably the social inferiors of those who employed them. In his famous work on the history of childhood, Philippe Ariès has speculated that wet-nurses may originally have been servants in the household, and it does seem that the

4. *Catherine Leslie, Countess of Melville*, 1691, by Sir John Medina. (In the Collection of the Earl of Leven and Melville.)

family in a country mansion would employ a servant, a servant's wife or the wife of a tenant. In the towns, it was usual to hire the wife of a tradesman, or perhaps a woman in from the country. In this way, the Laird of Barcaldine's son, John Campbell, sent for the local miller's wife who 'hes milk and is [a] good, cleanly woman' when his daughter was born, and successive wet-nurses employed by James Boswell in the 1770s were the wives of a tailor, a sawyer and a day-labourer.[18]

Although most medical men thought that the woman chosen should be young, in practice it seems that many mothers were willing to consider an older person. In the 1690s the Countess of Melville was recommending for her grandson a nurse who was 'six wicks [ago] broght to bed of a daughter. She is 36 yiers old and hath had fyve bairns, two of them is dead. She is a wiell favoured woman, very lean. You may cause the doctor com hier and sie her milk if you be not provyded alredy'.[19] Testing the milk, usually by squeezing a drop or two on to the fingernail, was an accepted procedure, for as one writer had said, it must be neither 'blackish, bluish, grey or reddish, neither sour, sharp, salty or brackish'.[20]

Once a suitable woman had been selected, she was installed in her employer's household, along with her own baby, and there she was treated as a very superior servant. Her quarters in the nursery were comfortable and a great deal of attention was given to her diet, which was to include plenty of nourishing meat, vegetables, milk and bread.[21] Because of her importance, she was paid a far higher wage than that received by the other servants, and when friends of the family visited the household and were taken to admire the baby, they invariably gave the nurse a lavish tip.[22]

Parents always hoped that the nurse would prove satisfactory and that she would stay, but there were often problems. In the autumn of 1540 Mary of Guise was distressed to find that the wet-nurse employed for her son, Prince James, could no longer continue in her service, for the simple reason that her milk had dried up. A replacement was found, but the baby was ill for several days afterwards.[23] The Dowager Countess of Mar was confronted with a similar problem in 1707. Her daughter-in-law died not long after giving birth to a son, and the older lady was left with the task of caring for the infant. After a good deal of trouble she found a suitable nurse, but a few week later she was reporting distractedly, 'I'm mightilie perplexed about dear Tomie's nurse, for I was in some hopes that it would have returned, her milk, I mean, come to her again, but these several days I'm out of all hopes, for it's like to go quite away, so I'm searching everiewhere for another'. Dr. Archibald Pitcairn came to her rescue and provided a substitute, but after a few months the new nurse fell downstairs and the Countess's troubles began all over again.[24]

By the Countess's time, there was a new development in the pattern of wet-nursing, for various families now chose to send their child out to the home of the nurse, rather than bringing her to their household. Even so, noble families usually adhered to the previous custom, for a variety of reasons. Considerations of status naturally made them prefer that their child should be reared in a socially suitable environment. After all, if the heir to a peerage spent the first months of his life in a humble cottage, there was no knowing what undesirable habits he might adopt. Worse still, the mortality among babies sent out in this way was notoriously high. All too many of them died as a result of lack of hygiene, careless treatment or overlaying in the night, and when that happened there was even the danger that the frightened nurse might try to substitute another baby in an attempt to conceal the tragedy.[25]

By keeping the wet-nurse in their own household, the wealthier families ensured that both she and the child were under close supervision and there was also less likelihood that he would grow up with a strong attachment to the nurse and little feeling for his natural mother, another cause for concern. An added advantage was that the nurse's husband was denied sexual access to her, thereby preserving her milk untainted. That was the theory of it, at least, but in practice it was not always possible to ensure the nurse's abstention. In 1697 Isobel Gordon, nursing the child of Robert Forbes in the parish of Coul, formed an illicit liaison with a fellow-servant, and eventually eloped with him on the night the baby was weaned.[26]

Examples such as these suggest that wet-nursing was fairly widespread in Scotland by the end of the seventeenth century, but it is impossible to attempt a quantitative analysis for either the seventeenth or the eighteenth century because of the lack of sources. However, some useful indications are to be found in the poll tax records of 1694. Imposed by an act of parliament in the previous year, the tax was collected from everyone except children under sixteen and people living on charity. The surviving rolls and returns are, for the most part, too fragmentary or too laconic to be helpful, but those of several Edinburgh parishes are amazingly complete, forming what the editor of two of the sets has called 'practically a census of the inhabitants'.[27] The records for the parishes of the Tolbooth Kirk, Old Kirk, College Kirk, Tron Kirk and Canongate Kirk are particularly useful for present purposes because they do include young children, often specifying the name, age and even the location of the child if he is away from home. The general context makes it clear that the term 'nurse' invariably refers to a wet-nurse, and in the discussion which follows, a small number of the children, although not actually stated as being with a wet-nurse, almost certainly were and have therefore been included.

In the five parishes, some 1,078 families had children. This number is an approximation, since it is not always possible to tell the age of sons and

5. *Dr. Archibald Pitcairn,* by Sir John Medina.
(In the Collection of the Royal College of Surgeons.)

daughters, but it is reasonably accurate. Of these families, seventy-three (or 6.8%) either employed a wet-nurse in their household or sent a child out to one. Tolbooth Kirk Parish had the highest number of wet-nurses: 12% of the families with children employed them, while Canongate had the lowest percentage at 1.8. The reason for the difference appears to be a social one. Tolbooth Kirk Parish had a large number of upper middle-class households employing several servants. In the Canongate, there were more small tradesmen and working-class people who did not keep a servant at all, let alone an expensive wet-nurse.

The social division is also reflected in the occupations of the fathers who employed wet-nurses. No fewer than 43% of those whose occupations are known were merchants and 31% were lawyers. Gentlemen accounted for 8% and a further 4% were doctors, including Dr. Archibald Pitcairn himself. One or two other professional men are to be found on the list — a minister and a soldier — then there were solitary examples of tradesmen such as a candle-maker, a baker, a periwig maker and a skinner. While it would be dangerous to generalise from such a small

sample, it does seem probable that in Scotland, as elsewhere, the practice of wet-nursing was gradually spreading downwards in society.

While on the subject of social class, it is also worth considering the occupations of those fathers who kept their children at home, compared with those who put them out to nurse. Of the total of seventy-three families, forty-one took the nurse in to the household while thirty-two sent the children out. On the whole, lawyers were more likely to keep the baby at home: 70% of their number did so, as did all three doctors and all four gentlemen. Slightly more than half the merchants followed suit, the figure being 52%. Considering the tradesmen as a group, only 25% had the nurse in, while 75% sent the child out. This would imply that social class was again a determining factor and that the wealthier or more status-conscious families followed the example of the aristocracy. No doubt the reasons were practical too: it was not only much more expensive to pay the nurse to move in, but she and her baby required extra accommodation which not everyone could provide. Incidentally, family size does not seem to have influenced the decision to employ a nurse, though there is a suggestion that people with larger families were more likely to send the child out. Of the forty-one who had the nurse in, 44% had only one or two children, whereas of the thirty-two who sent the child out, the figure was 34%.

General trends apart, various interesting details emerge from the poll tax records. The fee paid to the nurse is quite often stated, and it ranged from under £10 Scots a year to just over £100. Where the rates are known, 66% of the nurses were receiving £50 a year or less, but if this seems low it must be set in the context of the wages paid to other female servants in the same household. This shows that 95% of the wet-nurses had at least twice as much as the other women servants, 40% of them had four times more and 20% had at least five times as much. Profession of the father does not seem to have affected the rate so much as individual generosity or otherwise.

We do not know how much was paid to the nurses who kept children in their homes, although the location is often stated. Three of the babies mentioned in the tax records were 'in town', but most were either said to be 'in the country' or in small villages on the edge of Edinburgh — Colinton, Swanston, Ravelston and Cramond. One or two who were further afield in Dalkeith, Lauder and Kirkliston were probably with relatives. It was not surprising to find that David Scott of Scotstarvit, a Fife gentleman, had 'a child in the toun of Crail'. While any conclusions drawn from such limited material can only be tentative, the evidence does suggest that parents were sending their children out to the healthier air of the country, but keeping them where possible within visiting distance. There are certainly mentions elsewhere of parents going to see their children at nurse: in 1671 Sir John Lauder of Fountainhall had given his wife two and half dollars 'when she went to Waughton to sie hir son', an infant.[28]

Some parents had more than one child out at nurse, and it was not always the youngest member ·of the family who was away from home. Richard Brown, candlemaker in Tolbooth Kirk parish, had three children. Robert, aged three, was at home, eighteen-month-old Margaret was 'at present in the country' but Isobel, born just twelve days earlier, was still at home. The mother's health may have accounted for such differences, or it could be that a family waited for a few weeks before finding a suitable nurse. Normally, an infant was weaned at a year or eighteen months, but some are known to have remained with their nurse after weaning had taken place. Finally the records give a little information about the social status of the wet-nurses themselves. One was the wife of a maltman, another was married to a mason, a third was a servant's wife and a fourth was the wife of a soldier.

Such was the pattern in Edinburgh, but what was the situation elsewhere? At first sight it might appear that wet-nurses scarcely existed outside the large towns. The poll tax records for West Lothian, Midlothian and Renfrewshire are satisfyingly complete, yet the only nurse mentioned in any of these areas was employed by the Laird of Houston and his wife, who had five children and paid their nurse £40 a year compared with the £16 received by their other female servants. Of course, it could be that the records do not differentiate in terminology between nurse and servant, but from the fees paid it seems clear that none of the 'servitrixes' was a nurse.[29]

All the same, it would be rash to assume that no wet-nursing took place. The evidence remains tantalisingly scarce, but significant details can be found. In 1614, for example, when John Hendrie, collier in Little Fawside, admitted setting fire to a coal mine, it was revealed that he had been helped by Elspeth Hadden who was 'servand and nureis to John Levingstoun and fosterit [i.e. suckled]to him an bairne'. The following year, on 12th October, 1615, the burgh court of Kirkcudbright ordered Grisel McCartney to pay £4 Scots 'to Malie Moffatt, quhilk scho promissit for burding of hir nureis and barne'.[30]

In part, the increasing use of wet-nurses along with advances in medical knowledge accounted for the renewed public controversy about infant feeding in the eighteenth century. Horrified at the high rate of child mortality associated with wet-nursing, Dr. William Cadogan in 1748 published an influential essay urging mothers to breast-feed if they possibly could, then in 1762 Rousseau made his famous protest against wet-nursing in *Emile*. Scottish writers were not slow to join in the debate. 'It is the duty of the mother to nurse her own child,' thundered Lord Kames, declaring that 'even the most delicate court lady would take delight in it were not her manners corrupted by idleness and dissipation', while George Chapman the educationist was in no doubt that 'it is a duty incumbent on mothers to suckle their children, if they be able to effect it'.[31] Chapman urged that the newborn child be put to the breast 'even though the mother should not appear to have milk; for the sucking of the child brings the milk', but for the most part the eighteenth-century writers were saying nothing new. They stressed the nutritional and emotional advantages of maternal suckling, but in so doing they were merely repeating the arguments put by Bartholomew of England in the thirteenth century and Eucharius Roesslin in the sixteenth. What gave a new edge to their remarks was that they were now admonishing ladies of fashion, and their criticism of wet-nursing was just part of their general condemnation of women's alleged desertion of their natural role in life.

It is true that the role of upper and middle-class women in society was changing in eighteenth-century Scotland, in that the lady of leisure was now replacing the active mistress of the household. Moreover, this undoubtedly affected not only how women were treated but how they saw themselves.[32] Margaret, Countess of Dumfries, for instance, wrote to tell Lord Kames that although she supported his views, she feared that the very 'women of fashion' who would most benefit were probably too delicate to bear the fatigue of breast-feeding and thought that instead 'a more robust woman' should be employed. 'Were the choice mine I would attempt it,' she explained earnestly, 'tho I was once so unlucky as not to succeed'.[33]

The countess was perfectly sincere in her comments. To this day, writers on child-rearing have tended to see wet-nursing as a sign of maternal indifference, a form of institutionalised abandonment,[34] yet to anyone studying the documents of the time it is clear that most women handed their children over to a nurse in the genuine belief that it was the best if not the only course of action they could take. If their good intentions all too often had fatal consequences, those were the outcome of ignorance rather than wilful indifference.

Acknowledgements
References to Justiciary Records appear with the approval of the Keeper of the Records of Scotland, and quotations from Crown-copyright material with the permission of the Controller of H.M. Stationery Office. I am also grateful to the private owners of the archives quoted and of the pictures used as illustrations, for permission to include them.

References
1. W. Fraser, *Memorials of the Montgomeries* (Edinburgh 1859), i, 207.
2. *Foreign Correspondence with Marie de Lorraine, Queen of Scotland, from the Originals in the Balcarres Papers* ed. Marguerite Wood (Scottish History Society 1923-5, hereafter cited as *Balcarres Papers*), i, 51-2; *Calendar of State Papers Relating to Scotland and to Mary, Queen of Scots 1547-1603* ed. J. Bain and others (Edinburgh 1898-), ii, 289.
3. R. H. Cromek, *Remains of Nithsdale and Galloway Song* (London 1910), 310-13; *The English and Scottish Popular Ballads* ed. Francis J. Child (New York 1965), i, 358-9; *cf.* Lowry Charles Wimberly, *Folklore in the English and Scottish Ballads* (New York 1965), 326-8. I am grateful to Dr. Emily B. Lyle for drawing my attention to the ballad material.
4. Mary Martin McLaughlin, 'Survivors and Surrogates: Children and Parents from the Ninth to the Thirteenth Centuries', in Lloyd de Mause, *The History of Childhood* (U.S.A. 1974), 115; Lawrence Stone, *The Family, Sex and Marriage in England 1500-1800* (London 1977), 6.
5. De Mause, *op.cit.*, 115.
6. *Harys Wallace* ed. M. McDiarmid (Scottish Text Society 1968), i, lines 273-5.
7. National Library of Scotland, Yester Papers, Acc. 4862, Box 8, Fla; *The best of our owne: letters of Archibald Pitcairne 1652-1713* ed. W. T. Johnston (Edinburgh 1979), 35; W. Fraser, *The Red Book of Grandtully* (Edinburgh 1868), ii, 325-6.
8. M. J. Tucker, 'The Child as Beginning and End: Fifteenth and Sixteenth Century Childhood', in de Mause, *op.cit.*, 243; Elisabeth W. Marvick, 'Nature versus Nurture: Patterns and Trends in Seventeenth-Century French Child-Rearing', in *ibid.*, 264-6; G. F. Still, *The History of Paediatrics* (Oxford 1931), 185-6, quoting Hew Chamberlen's translation of François Mauriceau, *Traité des Maladies des Femmes Grosses* (London 1683).
9. Henry N. Paul, *The Royal Play of Macbeth* (New York 1950), 388-90.
10. Morwenna and John Rendle-Short, *The Father of Child Care: Life of William Cadogan 1711-97* (Bristol 1966), 25, quoting Daniel Defoe, *The Complete English Gentleman.*
11. *Boswell, Laird of Auchinleck* ed. J. W. Reed and F. A. Pottle (Yale 1977), 248.
12. *Personal Recollections from Early Life to Old Age of Mary Somerville, with selections from her correspondence* ed. Martha Somerville (Edinburgh 1873), 9.
13. Alexander Carlyle, *Anecdotes and Characters of the Time* (Oxford University Press 1973), 228.
14. D.H.S.S. Report, *Breast Feeding* (London 1978), 2-25.
15. *William Hay's Lectures on Marriage* ed. John C. Barry (Edinburgh 1967), 153.
16. Scottish Record Office (S.R.O.), Dalhousie Muniments, GD45/26/149.
17. Still, *op.cit.*, 185-6; Nicholas Culpeper, *A Directory for Midwives* (Edinburgh 1668), 136-8.
18. Philippe Ariès, *Centuries of Childhood,* translated by Robert Baldick (London 1962), 374; S.R.O., Campbell of Barcaldine Papers, GD170/793/28A; *Boswell: The Ominous Years 1774-1776* ed. C. Ryskamp and F. A. Pottle (Yale 1963), 164, 174, 175; *Boswell, Laird of Auchinleck 1778-82* ed. Joseph W. Reed and F. A. Pottle (Yale 1977), 12.
19. S.R.O., Leven and Melville Papers, GD26/13/417/34.
20. De Mause, *op.cit.*, 243, quoting Eucharius de Roesslin, *Byrth of Mankynde.*
21. George Chapman, *A Treatise on Education* (London 1784), 124.
22. E.g. Hamilton Archives, 560/5.
23. *Balcarres Papers,* i, 51-2.
24. S.R.O., Mar and Kellie Papers, GD124/15/552/1, 7; GD124/15/512/4, 6, 7, 12.
25. De Mause, *op.cit.*, 34; Stone, *op.cit.*, 100.
26. S.R.O., Register of Consistorial Decreets, Edinburgh, CC8/5/1 ff. 546-54.
27. *Edinburgh Poll Tax Returns for 1694* ed. Marguerite Wood (Scottish Record Society 1951), 14; S.R.O., Poll Tax Records, E70/4/1, 5, 6, 7, 9.
28. *Journals of Sir John Lauder, Lord Fountainhall* ed. Donald Crawford (Scottish History Society 1900), 251.
29. S.R.O., Poll Tax Records, E70/13, 8, 12.

30. S.R.O., Justiciary Records, small papers, JC26/7. Dr. Margaret H. B. Sanderson kindly drew my attention to this document; *Kirkcudbright Town Council Records 1606-58* ed. John, 4th Marquis of Bute and C. Armet (privately printed 1958), i, 177.

31. William Cadogan, *An Essay upon Nursing and the Management of Children* (London 1748); Jean Jacques Rousseau, *Emile ou de l'Education* edd. F. and P. Richard (Paris 1939); Lord Kames, *Loose Hints upon Education* (Edinburgh 1782), 33-44; Chapman, *op.cit.*, 123.

32. Rosalind K. Marshall, *Virgins and Viragos: A History of Women in Scotland 1080-1980* (London 1983), 167-87.

33. S.R.O., Moray of Abercairny Muniments, GD24/1/589.

34. Stone, *op.cit.*, 6, 194, 100; de Mause, *op.cit.*, 34-5; Ariès, *op.cit.*, 374.

Tenements: A Pre-Industrial Urban Tradition

P Robinson

The ubiquitous tenements, the walk-ups of the burghs and cities, represent a flat tradition that Scots have at best taken for granted and at worst actively sought to destroy. Their association with the 'bad old days' has often been intense, especially in the west, and yet the poor image conceals a practice of living off the ground which continues with the multi-storey flat and can be traced back almost five centuries. It is as if the tenements have represented something that is not quite respectable: an ugly reminder of the past, to be concealed rather than investigated and discussed. Even Scots familiar with the genre would hardly describe the grimness and barrack-like appearance of many of the survivors as attractive; although it has to be said in mitigation that some of these past associations are being steadily redeemed by recent improvements, which are revealing unexpected detail and colour from under a century of grime.

The tenement reputation may also have something to do with our prejudices being generated south of the border, where the very word can conjure up even starker images of Peabody Buildings, paternalism and poverty. Certainly flat life in England has been a relatively recent experience, and for many people outside London, Northumberland and Tyneside it does not go back any further than the multi-storey flat, with all that implies.

From this recent experience of high-rise on both sides of the border it would be hardly controversial to deduce that people are not generally predisposed towards living off the ground. Why then was the practice reported as commonplace in small towns and villages in Scotland and Northumberland in the 1720s? And why did all ranks of society tolerate accommodation in tenement flats up to fourteen floors high in late seventeenth century Edinburgh? It must also be said that they were living in conditions of some discomfort, without water supply or sanitation, and they were faced with the ever present risk of fire and collapse.

Local custom, perhaps an aberration? The evidence would seem to bear this out, but the most fascinating question raised by the tenement tradition is the light it casts on the power of ingrained habit in influencing the way we live. Even now few towns are without at least one massive Victorian or Edwardian tenement block, and they still give the larger burghs and cities their distinctive character, notwithstanding an energetic half century of slum clearance. Why did a pre-industrial tradition with so many apparent disadvantages become so established in the mind of the urbanised Scot, so as to become in turn almost a symbol of Scotland's industrial success and decline?

Tracing the fortunes of the Scottish flat tradition offers some clues as to why it should have occurred in the first place and why the tenement habit should have persisted. To do this is to cut a rough path through Scottish urban history. Necessarily it means examining trends over a long interval of time, rather than looking at particular buildings in any detail, and inevitably as many questions are raised as are answered. The story divides into two quite distinct phases; the pre-industrial beginnings dealt with in this paper, and an industrial legacy which was the product of different forces.

Some Basic Definitions

For those unfamiliar with the building type, the popular understanding of 'tenement' in Scotland is of a massive Victorian or Edwardian stone structure of between three and five storeys in height containing up to twenty or so flats. These flats are reached by a common passage, universally referred to as a 'close', and a stair. Variations on this general theme can be considerable. In Glasgow, tenements are rarely more than four storeys high and are without an attic. A typical example is shown in Figure 1. Dundee tenements are of three or four floors, but sometimes

These are no more than broad outlines of four important types, but they serve to demonstrate the variety of structures that can be found across Scotland. The real picture is complex, as more formal definitions and local usage embrace buildings which go well beyond the stereotypes. These include the two storey and two storey and attic 'cottage flats', or 'stacked cottages' of the smaller burghs, which some city dwellers might not recognise as 'tenements' in their terms.[1] South of the border the word has a somewhat different meaning, referring to what Scots would call a subdivided, or 'made-down' house.

In medieval usage, 'tenement' embraced all forms of proprietorship or occupation of real, in the sense of 'real estate', property; so that both a piece of land and a building could be referred to as a 'tenement'. Only much later did it come to be applied more specifically to 'a building constructed or adapted to be let in portions to a number of tenants, with each separately occupied portion being regarded as an individual dwelling'.[2] The contemporary Scottish legal definition of a tenement is 'a building containing a number of dwelling houses within four walls, all or a number of them having a common access from the street and so structurally divided and separated as to be capable of being distinct property or a distinct subject of lease'.[3] In a curious reversal of terms the word 'land' is applied to a building, usually urban, and often with the prefix 'fore-' or 'back-' added, depending on the part of the structure identified.

'Close' initially referred to the enclosed and cultivated ground behind the 'fore-land'. It was a 'closour', literally an enclosure. The close only came to mean a passage when the burgages, that is the long, narrow, cultivated strips of ground occupied by the burgesses, or freemen of the burghs, were built up and became filled with 'backlands'.[4] Figures 2 and 3 show diagrammatically how some of these terms were changing between the early and late medieval periods.

At the turn of the fifteenth century, 'flet' was being used in Scotland to describe the inner part of a house.[5] By 1800 'flet' had come to refer to the complete floor or storey of a building, and only more recently has it come to be used in the more familiar context of a suite of rooms forming a complete dwelling. Although the word has Old English origins, until well into the last century its general usage was confined to Scotland.[6] 'Flat', therefore, could be regarded as a Caledonian contribution to our common

1. Typical working-class Glasgow tenement of 1900: 104 Gourlay Street, Springburn, Glasgow (now demolished). It contained 12 houses; 4 single ends and 8 room and kitchens.

with an attic storey. Flats are reached from a circular 'turnpike' stair protruding into the back court and by open galleries running out from the stair at each floor: the 'platties' as they are known locally. Edinburgh tenements are taller, occasionally with as many as five floors, plus an attic and a basement. The Georgian New Town survivors tend to have a straight stair and landings immediately behind the front elevation and this is usually visible from the street. Later examples are more likely to have a dark internal stair lit by a rooflight, or 'cupola' in local usage. Close doors and 'main door flats', that is ground-floor houses reached directly from the street, are virtually universal in all classes of property in the capital. Aberdeen follows the Glasgow plan, but the tenements are more likely to have three floors and an attic, and behind the glistening granite outer walls the internal stairs and partitions are usually of timber.

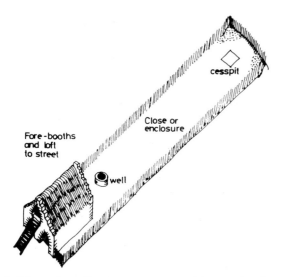

2. The early medieval tenement, comprising two booths and loft to the street with a close, or closout, behind containing cesspool and well. The boundaries would have been defined by withies and stakes.

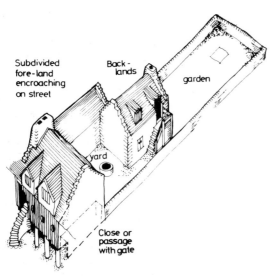

3. The late medieval tenement comprising sub-divided foreland with forestair encroaching on the street and with boarded timber gallery. The close has become a passage leading to a yard, backland and garden.

Anglo-Saxon culture and language. It must also be remembered that in Scotland 'flats' are often described as 'houses'.

Why Flats?

Crowding within a confined boundary is an obvious starting point if one is seeking to explain the origins of the flat, and it is tempting to look no further than Scotland's burgh traditions in developing this theme. Burghs were, after all, privileged trading enclaves deriving an income from the levying of customs and dues. They were part of an organised mercantile system, administered by burgesses, whose rights depended on their living and working within fixed boundaries, which were themselves necessary to regulate trade. Indeed the very word burgh comes from 'Burgus', literally a fortified enclosure.[7]

It is possible to argue that if the boundaries had been closely defined in relation to a burgh's population, then this in itself would explain a flat tradition developing in that particular place as a population increased over an interval of time. There is a certain attractiveness in this argument, but it is unlikely to have been a sufficient condition in Scotland, as even the more prestigious Royal Burghs were small and almost rural in character by present-day standards. Glasgow in 1450 is thought to have had a population of only 1,500.[8] Stirling in 1477 had only 120 burgesses, giving an estimated population of something like 750-800, and by the middle of the sixteenth century there were only 336 male adults in the Burgh.[9] At a weapon-showing in 1572, Peebles had only 140 men, and tax figures dating from the early seventeenth century suggest only 133 householders.[10] There could be no question of a spontaneous flat tradition developing under these circumstances if it were to be the product of crowding alone.

We also have the meticulous observations of Daniel Defoe, prompted by his arrival in Mordington just inside Berwickshire, on a journey north in the early 1720s. It is both a vital clue to the extent to which living off the ground, or more technically living off the solum, was prevalent at that time in Scotland, and it is a prompt to other explanations:

> The first Town we come to is as perfectly Scots as if it were 100 miles North of Edinburgh; nor is there the least Appearance of any Thing English either in Customs, Habits, Usages of the People, or in their Way of Living, Eating, Dress or Behaviour ... On the contrary, you have in England an abundance of Scotsmen, Scots Customs, Words, Habits and Usages, even more than becomes them; nay even the Buildings of the Town and the Villages imitate the

Scots almost all over Northumberland; witness their building the Houses with the Stairs (to the second Floor) going up on the Outside of the House, so that one Family may live below and another above, without going in at the same Door; which is the Scots Way of Living, and which we see in Alnwick and Warkworth, and several other towns . . .[11]

In Webster's Census thirty years later, Mordington had a population of 181 and a mysterious thirty six and one-fifth 'fighting men'.[12] As with the Royal Burghs there could be no question of crowding, and one has to look elsewhere for an explanation.

In one sense the Northumbrians *were* Scots, as Northumbria had been a disputed territory claimed by both kingdoms. That part north of the Tweed had fallen to Scotland during the tenth and eleventh centuries but it remained difficult to govern even in more settled times. Lawlessness in the Border country, as over much of Scotland, persisted until almost within living memory of Defoe's day. Was it a simple search for security that led that part of the population with any measure of choice to live as far above the ground as they could afford? The defensible farm building, the bastle, was common in rural Northumberland a century earlier, and its principal defensive feature was domestic accommodation on the first-floor level above the solum, with access via a removable ladder.[13] No obvious trace remains of the buildings Defoe described in present-day Alnwick or Warkworth, but in nearby industrial Amble, several two-storey cottage flats survive dating from the mid-nineteenth century − a pointer to the existence in the area of a pre-industrial model, as well as a hint towards the origins of the better known 'Tyneside flat'.

Fortified Boundaries

Crowding and security, as well as habit, all feature in at least two past explanations of the Scottish flat tradition. When William Chambers described the sanitary condition of the Old Town of Edinburgh to the Poor Law Commissioners in 1840, he spoke of it as '. . . built in a compact manner within walls; story was piled on story, with a view of saving room, and so closely were jammed the numerous closes or alleys diverging from the main thoroughfare, that in many cases a person might step from the window of one house to the window of the house opposite. What was

begun from necessity has continued from mere usage'.[14] The Royal Commission on Housing in Scotland, reporting in 1918, took a generally similar view:

The tenement of three, four, and, in certain cases, five or more storeys represents the final development of housing during the nineteenth century and in the great majority of the larger Scots burghs. It is important to understand what led to this line of development, so different from the two-storey self-contained cottages which form the prevailing type in English Towns . . . If we look to the city of Edinburgh for illustration of such causes, we find an ancient walled city, extending from the Castle to Holyrood, and comprising the Lawnmarket, with the few cross streets and the multitudinous narrow closes which fill in the intervening belt of land. Each of those closes is practically a street in itself fronted or closely hemmed in by tall tenements − centuries old − and at one time, in many cases, the resort and abode of fashion and society. Unable to extend for fear of attack from the south, whilst upon the north the city was water-bound and rock bound the growing population of the city could only expand skywards; hence, no doubt, those thickly-built closes and their many storied tenements. Upon this agglomeration − reared under such straits − there followed the districts of West Port and High Riggs, Potterrow and Pleasance, Richmond Street and the suburb of St. Leonard's, all of them now the abode of the labouring class; taking their type from the tenements of the ancient city, and seeming to impress the stamp of perpetuity upon the tenement as the pattern of the City's future building growth. The modern reproductions of the tenement plan, which may be seen in the working-class suburbs of Tynecastle, Gorgie, Restalrig, Easter Road, etc., are not like their prototype − the product of necessity, but that of choice and evil example, from which it appears difficult to depart. The early example of the tenemented system, so set in the Scottish capital, would appear to have given other Scottish towns the type for their copy in the soaring flats which have acquired for the towns of Scotland this particular and unenviable and distinctive feature. To the explanation in the last sentence it should probably be added that the example of Edinburgh has been reinforced by that of certain other ancient walled cities, e.g. Stirling, where similar conditions produced the same effect, and these may also be seen in very many Continental cities, where building space was limited by the circuit of the city walls'.[15]

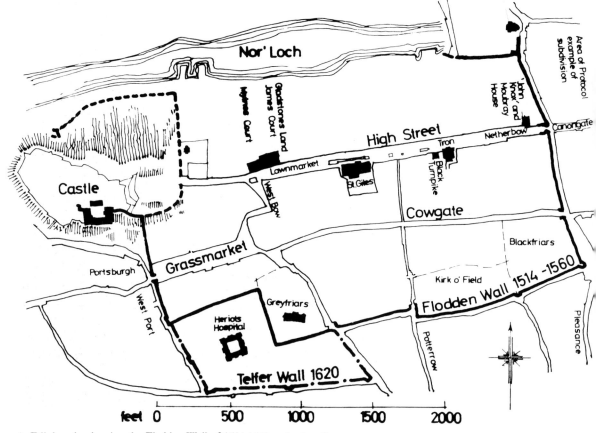

4. Edinburgh, showing the Flodden Wall of 1514-1560 and other features.

Edinburgh

There is no doubt that Edinburgh, through a combination of geography and circumstances, proved to be the exceptional burgh as far as crowding was concerned. The familiar crag-and-tail site would have been spacious enough in 1100, but by the later Middle Ages it had developed inflexible boundaries. To the north there was the so-called River Tumble, later dammed to form the Nor' Loch, and to the south there were in medieval terms the large monastic institutions of Blackfriars, 'Kirk o' Field', and Greyfriars.[16] The only clear path to expansion was taken up in the east by the separate burgh of Canongate, and to the west development was hindered by the steep descent to the Grassmarket through the West Bow (Figure 4).

The wars with England after 1285 led to the walling of the town and to significant changes in status, as it became, in the course of the 1400s, the permanent seat of Scottish Government. By 1535 the Court of

Session met regularly in Edinburgh, and noblemen, landowners, judges and lawyers became an enduring element in the population to compete for house room with those merchants and tradesmen whose livelihoods depended on their residence. Edinburgh became larger and more prosperous, as well as more sophisticated and a consumer centre in its own right. All this would have further stimulated manufacture and trade. It was a gradual process which profoundly changed the character of the City. As the principal burgh of the kingdom, it was where the fashionable lived for a least a part of the year, and if all roads led from Edinburgh, then this would be important in the diffusion of fashion and ideas.

The changed status was reflected in the population of what is generally referred to as the Ancient Royalty and which for practical purposes we can define as the area within the Flodden Wall. Of course evidence is scanty, but by making crude assumptions it is possible to follow an unmistakable upward trend. At

5. Houses of a type similar to those described by Robert Chambers in the Edinburgh Cowgate. He believed these houses to date from 1490 or 1500. From Grant's *Old and New Edinburgh*.

the time of the Sexcentenary celebrations in 1929, the (then) Frank Mears estimated the population at the time of the Bruce Charter in 1329 to be in the region of 2,000, based on a crude assessment of burgage plots.[17] For the sake of argument one could use this as a simple base line. By 1560 it had risen to 10,000,[18] an increase by a factor five. In 1635 there were nearly 4,000 entries recorded in the Stent Roll, representing a population of around 20,000, and an increase by a factor of ten.[19]

Sub-Division

The division of a tenement of land on the south side of the Canongate in February 1491 into three equal parts is described in the Protocol Book of James Young. This could be taken as typical of a continuing process of division made necessary by a combination of pressure of numbers, inheritance and the insistence in the ancient burgh laws that burgesses should be property owners.[20] In this instance the tenement

comprised a fore-land, made up of easter and wester fore-booths, and a fore-loft, later described as the 'upper storey', from which we might deduce that it was a two-storey structure. A backland, gardens and yards are also described. The sub-division was carried out with care. Each party received an element of the fore-land (the easter and wester booths and the upper storey respectively), and they each received a portion of the back property.[21] Clearly the process of sub-division was by that time taking place upwards as well as outwards.

More than 350 years later Robert Chambers was able to describe houses in the Cowgate which he believed to date from 1490 to 1500. The example he chose to illustrate, on the south side of the Cowgate opposite the foot of Mint Close, was a two-storey building corresponding closely to the Canongate model. He observed that the 'two booths, or shops, with gallery above (arrangement) conforms to the description of a tenement in Perth which was granted

a little before the year 1200 to the Church of Scone'. [22]
Chambers also refers to the slightly more prestigious
houses surviving elsewhere on the Canongate,
described as being located 'next below the Horse
Wynd'. 'Here, beside the ground accommodation and
gallery floor with an outside stair, there is a
contracted second floor, having also a gallery in front,
with a range of small windows. On the gallery floor,
at the head of the outside stair, is a finely moulded
door, at the base of an inner or turnpike stair leading
up to the second floor'. [23] Houses of a type similar to
those described by Chambers are shown in Figure 5.

It was the turnpike stair more than any other single
innovation which made high levels of congestion
possible in sixteenth century Edinburgh. Quite
simply it allowed the upward growth of Chambers'
Horse Wynd tenement to continue as far as the
technology of the day would allow. There are several
references to buildings named after this feature, all of
some antiquity. The 'Black Turnpike', or the Auld
Bishop of Dunkeld's Ludging, which stood on the
south side of the High Street a few feet west of the
Tron Church and at the head of Peebles Wynd, is one
such building that has received attention, and it is
thought to have dated from the fifteenth century. [24]
To what extent the more recent drawings of this
ancient land reflect its original design must be a
matter for speculation, but the general arrangement
of a turnpike stair encroaching on the street and
giving access to timber galleries was an obvious
solution to building high and would lend itself to sub-
division. Although Chambers observed: 'It is not to
be supposed that buildings of this order were
common in Edinburgh at that period. It is rather to
be imagined that they were very rare'. [25] Figure 6
shows the Skene sketch of the Black Turnpike.
Timber galleries such as these, initially for access,
were soon built up in the sixteenth century to become
apartments in their own right. The so-called John
Knox's House, the adjacent Moubray House and
Huntly House in the Canongate are the only
survivors of this period of the great timber-fronted
lands.

Refinement of the Flat Theme
Once the principle of formalised multi-occupation
within a single vertically divided structure had been
established, with separate titles for each 'flet' within
the 'land', the idiom appears merely to have been

o. Skene sketch of the Black Turnpike at the head of
Peebles Wynd, as it existed prior to demolition in 1788.
Edinburgh Public Libraries.

refined through time. In Edinburgh the enduring
theme is one of more people demanding higher standards of accommodation within the fixed boundary of
the Flodden Wall. Lists of goods inherited suggest
that a sixteenth century house was sparsely furnished
and would have been typically small, even for the
relatively better-off. [26] Needs were simple and easily
met. As the wealth and prestige of the City grew in
the seventeenth century, separate rooms for particular
uses became more common, each room with a fireplace and other refinements. There were more
wealthier citizens with more goods to store and
display.

When civic pride became an issue for the first time
in the course of the seventeenth century, stone
replaced timber as the predominant building
material. It allowed the structures to be more massive
and for fireplaces with flues to be accommodated with
reasonable safety. Fire was an ever present hazard,
and good timber for building was getting scarce.

We know from the Stent Roll of 1635 that Gladstone's Land, then recently refaced in stone, was
jointly owned by Thomas Gladstaines and David
Jonkin, both merchants, while the front portion of the
land was divided into five taxable units. Four flats

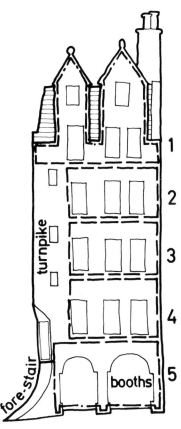

7. Division of Gladstone's Land frontage according to the Stent Roll, 1635.

were valued at £150 Scots and the fifth at £160 Scots (£12 Scots were worth £1 Sterling), with Thomas Gladstaines occupying the double top flat and David Jonkin the first floor above the shop at the foot of the turnpike.[27] The relative status of the occupiers can be judged from other entries in the same Roll. Dwellings in the close beneath were assessed at £20 Scots, while the wealthy Sir William Dick of Braid paid £500 and occupied a complete frontage on his own account, but his wealth and status were quite exceptional and should not be regarded as typical. Figure 7 suggests a division of Gladstone's Land based on these returns. Note that the turnpike stair starts at first-floor level above the forestair, like the Canongate examples, and does not extend to the ground in the manner of the Black Turnpike.

Evidence of purpose-built mansion flats for the well-to-do begins to appear in the second quarter of the seventeenth century. The rebuilding of the Parliament Close area following the fires of 1674 and 1676 was

acknowledged to be to the very highest standards, and the lands were occupied by some of Edinburgh's leading citizens.[28] These lands were in turn to be burned down in 1700 and again in 1824. Few hints survive to indicate how the earlier replacements looked, although they are thought to have had seven storeys towards Parliament Close and at least fourteen towards the Cowgate, where the ground dropped away sharply.

Mylne's Court at the top of the Lawnmarket dates from 1690 and remains an isolated survivor from a period of intense building activity. By any standards it is a massive structure, opening out onto a courtyard rather than a close. The wealthy were becoming more discriminating in their ways and fashion was beginning to show itself as important. Here the turnpike was abandoned in favour of a generous straight stair with half-landings, and the frontage to the High Street has a distinctly plain and modern look, sitting comfortably with the James Court High Street frontage dating from the 1790s. The less visible back elevation, however, remains craggy and medieval, maintaining some of the character of Gladstone's Land. The photograph in Figure 8, taken in the 1880s, shows a clear progression from the timber-fronted lands with forestairs, as at Lady Stair's Close and Baxter's Close, through Gladstone's Land to James Court. The frontages shown are those appearing on the Thomas Hamilton drawing on the North side of the Lawnmarket, dated 1830,[29] which clearly suggests that the James Court frontage survived at least the fire of 1857.

High and Dirty

Gordon's map may be more illustrative than accurate. Nevertheless, it is a striking picture of how the burgage plots had by 1647 been built up and the extent to which the buildings facing the High Street had grown in height (Figure 9). The fragment showing the area around St. Giles shows a clear difference in scale between the High Street and the Cowgate. Contemporary descriptions leave no doubt that Edinburgh was a crowded place and some, like Thomas Morer, an Englishman visiting the city in 1689, also give a good account of the buildings, noting that:

> Their old houses are cased with boards and have oval windows (without casements of glass), which they open or shut as it stands with their conveniency.

8. North side of the Lawnmarket, Edinburgh, *circa* 1880, showing (left to right) James' Court dating from 1720, Gladstone's Land, Lady Stair's Close and Baxter's Close. National Monuments record, courtesy of Mr Gerald Cobb.

Their new houses are made of stone, with good windows modishly framed and glazed, and so lofty, that five or six stories is an ordinary height, and one row of buildings that is near the Parliament Close with no less than fourteen. The reason is, their scantness of room, which not allowing 'em large foundations they are forced to make up in the super structure, to entertain comers, who are very desirous to be in, or as near to as they can to the city . . . Most of the houses, as they are parted into divers tenements, so they have as many landlords as stories; and therefore have no dependence on one another, otherwise as they stand on the same foundation so that in this respect they may be compared to our student's apartments at the Inns of Court, which are bought and sold without regard to the chambers above or below 'em.[30]

Other strangers may have spoken in admiring terms of the High Street, but the less genteel features of high density life also caught their attention; some, perhaps, more directly than they would have wished. 'High and Dirty' was the blunt appraisal of Thomas Kirk on his visit to Edinburgh ten years earlier.[31]

Although the Royal Court had left in 1603 for

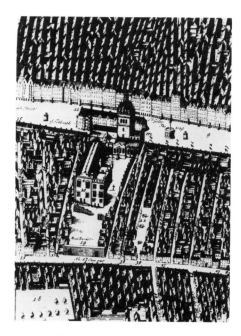

9. Fragment of Gordon's Map showing the area around St. Giles in 1647. Note the difference in scale between the High Street frontages and the Cowgate.

London, Edinburgh was still the administrative and official capital of Scotland. The Canongate, at that time outside the boundary of the Ancient Royalty, appears to have suffered most as the nobility lost interest in maintaining their houses on the approach to Holyrood. The more significant change came in 1707 with the departure of the Privy Council and Parliament for London. Despite these changes in status, the population of Edinburgh continued to rise within boundaries that had remained essentially unchanged since 1300. In 1694 the population has been calculated as being in the order of 27,000,[32] a thirteen fold increase over the notional 1329 baseline; and in 1755 Webster estimated the parish corresponding to the Ancient Royalty to contain approximately 31,000 people,[33] a fifteen fold increase.

The Picture Elsewhere

Necessity created the flat tradition in Edinburgh, but why it should occur elsewhere in less crowded burghs and villages is not quite so clear. Certainly, relatively high lands are recorded as existing in pre-industrial Dundee and Glasgow, and the similarities are sometimes striking. The three-storey Garland's Land, for example, dating from 1558 and illustrated in Lamb's Dundee, reflects the turnpike and gallery access idiom of the Black Turnpike, and this was also true of the slightly later Earl of Kinnoull's Lodging in Watergate, Perth, which was demolished in 1966.[34]

Only the Cathedral and the Provand's Lordship remain of Old Glasgow, but early drawings suggest that many of the houses on the High Street were of a type closely resembling the Edinburgh 'Land' and many were timber-fronted. They appear to have been smaller, never more than five stories, and rarely more than four. Glasgow may not have been pressed for space in quite the same way as the capital; even so the burgage plots appear to have been densely developed. Many of the old timber-fronted lands survived well into the nineteenth century in the closes and wynds, and they also bear a striking resemblance to their Edinburgh equivalents. That photographed by Thomas Annan in Nightingale Close in Glasgow's Saltmarket in 1868 shares the forestair and scale of the Edinburgh Cowgate (Figure 10), and might be compared with Chambers' descriptions and the Gordon map.

It is beyond doubt that multi-storey living had been established among the better-off over a long interval

10. Close No. 28 Saltmarket, Glasgow, showing a basically similar form to the Edinburgh Cowgate. Thomas Allan, 1868. Mitchell Library, Glasgow Collection.

of time in Edinburgh, and it is tempting to look no further than the diffusion argument in explaining the practice elsewhere, just as the Royal Commission had done in 1918. This reasoning, however, denies the possibility of self-generation and does not fit comfortably into the evidence of Defoe. One might speculate that the tastes and fashions of the capital were copied to at least some degree, and no doubt the popular conception of what constituted an urban dwelling would be coloured by the experience of Edinburgh, but diffusion does not offer a complete explanation.

Self-Generation

Some of the points raised in the Edinburgh analysis offer useful motives for sub-division elsewhere, with or without crowding. As long as burghs had distinct status, and the rights and privileges of individuals depended on land holding and residence within fixed boundaries, sub-division was likely to have continued. This goes some way to explaining why separate title should be given to property off the solum, like the loft in the Canongate example. Sub-division through inheritance falls into this same category, as does pressure for a frontage on a main thoroughfare, or market.

Another factor which cannot be ignored is the effect of relative poverty even among the better-off in medieval Scotland. This was something that early travellers observed from Froissart in the fourteenth century to Estienne Perlin in the sixteenth. The latter claimed that a merchant in Scotland with 400 livres was considered rich, while in England, Spain, Portugal, Germany and Flanders 1,200-1,500 livres would represent the income of a rich man. Poor weather and unsettled political conditions in the sixteenth century would have intensified a natural poverty.[35] Currency was substantially debased in sixteenth century Scotland and inflation continued well into the seventeenth, and this may have had the effect of increasing the price of house room just as today. These factors in themselves may have encouraged sub-division and a modest attitude towards accommodation even among the merchant classes. Merchants were, after all, one of the few social groups in a position to procure new urban building and dictate custom and fashion. They may have been poor in absolute terms (and poverty and sub-division have always gone hand in hand), but they were still a peer group.

All of these considerations may have had some influence on behaviour, but none is as powerful as the need in one form or another for defence and security in an unsettled country. This argument offers an attractive and plausible link between practices in relatively isolated communities, the larger burghs and Edinburgh in the period up to and after the union of the Crowns. A simple instinct for self-preservation helps to explain why people should wish to live above the solum in the first place, and this appears to be the key factor. We have seen that the crowding in Edinburgh in the period up to and after the Union of the Crowns. A simple instinct for self-preservation growth and development, but the very absence of external fortifications and a defensible boundary elsewhere also holds a clue. The palisaded ditches and mounds of the burghs may have been important boundaries of privilege, and of some utility in the day-to-day control of trade, but they would have been ineffective barriers to determined attackers. Poor as

provincial freemen may have been, they still had goods to secure, and one must suppose some instinct for their own safety. The only people in any position at all to influence the arrangement of new buildings were the relatively better-off, adding weight to this argument. In larger settlements with an established merchant community there would be a reasonable expectation of contact with other burghs, including Edinburgh and, to a lesser extent, Continental Europe through trade. In this sense prejudices once established would be continually reinforced by experiences elsewhere, as the 1918 Royal Commission had suggested.

A Pre-Industrial Flat Tradition

One might use this brief analysis of the pre-industrial picture to suggest several distinct stages of development, using the self-preservation argument as a starting point. Although it has to be acknowledged that this was not the only factor at work, it is a clear pointer to why the better-off should wish to live above the solum simultaneously in various parts of lowland Scotland and the Border country. The forestair, like the bastle ladder, offered some basic protection, and its use was clearly widespread. Living at least one floor up had other advantages in the damp Scottish climate, and this would be especially so in severe winter weather with unmade roads and poor drainage. There would have been practical advantages in 'living above the shop' in the burghs, and the 'two booths and loft' arrangement appears to have served well over a long interval of time.

Sub-division through inheritance, or for other reasons, such as satisfying the condition of property ownership or residence for the purpose of gaining a burgess ticket, might make the ground floors more acceptable, not only as booths and workshops, but also as dwellings. In more isolated and less sophisticated communities this might be induced out of a basic need for shelter in a subsistence economy. At some point ownership of one element of a simple structure might cease to be within the control of an extended family and title would move into other hands. Later evidence in Edinburgh suggests that the more prestigious dwellings were on top, furthest from the ground, another hint that it was the better-off who 'stayed on top', just as Thomas Gladstone had done in 1635. To this one might add the abundance of good stone, lending itself to the building of relatively large and secure structures which would be suitable for sub-division and which could satisfy the modest aspirations of a sparing merchant peer group.

In smaller burghs and village communities that might be the end of the process, but in the crowded circumstances of Edinburgh the basic theme, once established, could be repeated upwards, sub-division above sub-division. The need for security might help to explain why the turnpike in William Chambers' Cowgate example started at the first floor and not on the ground and why this theme is merely extended upwards in Gladstone's Land. Only in the rarer 'Black-Turnpike' model does the turnpike extend to the ground. At some point, however, between the refacing of Gladstone's land in 1613 and the building of Mylne's Court in 1690, in Edinburgh at least, fashion, display, comfort and convenience became the dominating forces, leading to the genesis of the 'tenement' forms we can begin to recognise in terms of the stereotypes. If the High Street frontage of James Court dates from the 1790s, then one could regard the process of refinement as complete by that time. At that point quite different factors had come into play in the period of town expansion and land speculation, but that is another story.

Notes and References

1. Frank Walker takes issue with this point of definition in his narrowly Glasgow interpretation of the word 'tenement'. See F. A. Walker, 'The Glasgow Grid', in ed. Thomas A. Markus, *Order in Space and Society*, Mainstream, Edinburgh, 1982, 155-199, 158.

2. *OED*.

3. *Scottish Judicial Dictionary*, 1946, 299.

4. *OED*.

5. Warrack and Grant, *Chambers' Scots Dictionary*, 1974 edition, 180.

6. *OED*.

7. *OED*.

8. Quoted in ed. M. D. Loebel, *Historical Towns*, Johns Hopkins Press, Baltimore (undated), 2.

9. Stirling Council Records; quoted in RCAMS, *Inventory, Stirlingshire*, Vol. II, HMSO, 1963, 16.

10. Peebles Chronicle; quoted in RCAMS, *Inventory, Peeblesshire*, Vol. I, HMSO, 12.

11. Daniel Defoe, *Tour Thro' The Whole Island of Great Britain*, Vol. III, G. Strahan, 1727, 6. I am indebted to Geoffrey Stell of RCAMS for drawing attention to this reference.

12. Ed. Jas. Gray Kyd, *Scottish Population Statistics, including Webster's Analysis of Population 1755*, Edinburgh,

Scottish Academic Press, 1975, 12.

13. H. G. Ramm, R. W. McDowall and E. Mercer, *Shielings and Bastles*, London HMSO, 1970.

14. Wm. Chambers, *Report on the Sanitary State of the Residences of the Poorer Classes in the Old Town of Edinburgh*, 1840, 1.

15. Cd. 8731, *Royal Commission on Housing in Scotland, Report, etc.*, Edinburgh, HMSO 1918, paras 396, 400 and 401, 449.

16. On the south side of Edinburgh the Blackfriars established a convent in 1230, and in the same century the 'Kirk o' Field' (the Church of St. Mary in the Field) was established nearby. Two hundred years later the Greyfriars built a church and convent to the south-west, so that the three religious establishments formed a continuous southern boundary to the Cowgate, at that time an exclusive southern suburb.

17. Mears assumed there to have been about 200 holdings fronting the High Street, with approximately 150 more in the Grassmarket and Cowgate. He assumed each plot to have been occupied by six people, giving a total population at around the time of the Bruce Charter of approximately 2,000. Quoted in *City of Edinburgh 1329-1929*, Oliver and Boyd, 1929, 375.

18. The population of Edinburgh at the time of the Reformation in 1560 has been established at 10,000. This figure was kindly provided by Dr. Walter Makey (the City Archivist), and was based on research by Dr. Michael Lynch (Department of Scottish History, University of Edinburgh).

19. Figures provided by Dr. Makey, based on the Stent Roll of 1635. The original Roll is held in the Edinburgh City Archives.

20. For burgess status see W. M. Mackenzie, *The Scottish Burghs*, Oliver and Boyd, Edinburgh and London, 1949, 141.

21. Ed. Gordon Donaldson, *Protocol Book of James Young, 1485-1515*, Scottish Record Society, 1942, item 410, 95-96.

22. Robert Chambers, *Edinburgh Papers*, Wm. and Robt. Chambers, London and Edinburgh, 1861, 2.

23. *Ibid.*, 4.

24. The Black Turnpike is briefly referred to in *City of Edinburgh 1329-1929*, 396-397, and more fully in the RCAMS *Edinburgh Inventory etc.*, 128. See also Boog-Watson Notes (Edinburgh City Library) and other sources. *Minor Antiquities*, Edinburgh, Wm. and Robt. Chambers, 1833, and The Edinburgh Inventory date the Black Turnpike as 1461 (xxi and 128 respectively); but the Boog-Watson Notes point to an earlier date of 1443 (Vol. 15, 100), although it is not clear on what evidence this is based.

25. *Minor Antiquities, op.cit.*, xxi-xxii.

26. See RCAMS, *Edinburgh Inventory etc.*, lxvii. This

cites the case of John Young, who in 1530 received a silver mazer and spoon, a plate, a pot, a quart stoup, a pint stoup, a table, a bed, an aumbry (a food store), a shrine, a chair and a form as the contents of a house.

27. Gladstone's Land, frontage to High Street. Extract from *Stent Roll 1635*, NW Quarter, 84.

28. See Dr. Marguerite Wood, 'All the Statlie Buildings of . . . Thomas Robertson; A Building Speculator of the Seventeenth Century', *The Book of The Old Edinburgh Club*, Vol. XXIV, 1942, 126-151. Also George Home, 'Notes on the Re-building of Edinburgh in the Last Quarter of the Seventeenth Century', in *Book of The Old Edinburgh Club*, Vol. 29, 1956, 111-142.

29. See F. C. Mears, 'Measured Drawings of Lawnmarket and Castlehill made by Thomas Hamilton, Architect', in *Book of The Old Edinburgh Club*, Vol. 25, T. and A. Constable, 1923, 249-250.

30. Peter Hume Brown, *Early Travellers in Scotland*, Facsimile Edition, Jas. Thin, Edinburgh, 1973, 279.

31. *Ibid.*, 256.

32. Estimated figure calculated by Dr. Makey on the basis of the Poll Tax returns of 1694. The principal reference to this tax is Dr. Marguerite Wood, 'Edinburgh Poll Tax Returns', in *Book of The Old Edinburgh Club*, Vol. XXV, 1945, 90-126.

33. Estimate based on Webster's Census. Considerable suburban expansion to the south and west of the Ancient Royalty makes the figures difficult to disaggregate. The total population of the City was calculated as of the order of 66,000, but only a portion resided within the ancient boundaries. Ref: ed. James Gray Kyd, *op.cit.*, 14-15.

34. The Earl of Kinnoull's Lodging was a three-storeyed stone building with a turnpike stair encroaching on the street and with gallery access to the upper floors. It is thought to have dated from 1600. RCAMS Ref. PTD/193/4.

35. Peter Hume Brown, *op.cit.*, 11, 76. This point is made in L. F. Grant, *The Social and Economic Development of Scotland Before 1603*, Oliver and Boyd, Edinburgh, 1930, 551.

Box-Beds and Bannocks. The Living Past

R H Buchanan

This paper* relates the study of folklife as it has developed in Britain to the folk museums which are now to be found in many places in these islands and elsewhere in Europe. The title is intended to reflect the scope of the subject, with its primary interest in studying the objects of everyday life: the furniture and food of the household, the implements and tools of the farmyard and craftsman's shop. Some of the artifacts we use today are modern inventions, like the electric toaster or the power drill; but many more are derived from a more remote past, and therein lies the value of their study for scholars in other disciplines — especially for economic historians and archaeologists. By watching how they were made, and more importantly how they were used, enigmatic artifacts found through excavation may sometimes be interpreted, and their use explained. As Charles Thomas puts it: '. . . folk life studies show the archaeologist not only the nature of what he has discovered, but also the extent of what he can never hope to recover'.[1] In particular, folklife studies try to place the artifact in context: the box-bed, for example, in relation to the house and to the social history of the families who used it. Folk tradition is an essential part of this study, as expressed in belief, speech, drama, dance and music; it is the anthropology of the past.

Box-beds and bannocks are objects of the living past which folklife scholars study, and which are seen as representative samples of the life of their particular community. But box-beds similar to those of Fife may also be seen much further away, for example in County Down across the Irish Sea, and in both north and south Holland. This point illustrates another facet of folklife study: the search for cultural relations between peoples and places as exemplified in familiar artifacts or in folk tradition. Sigurd Erixon, the Swedish founding-father of modern folklife studies,

regarded this search for cultural affinities as a primary aim of folklife research, an active contribution 'to a better reciprocal knowledge and understanding between the peoples and [to] further the possibilities of international reconciliation'.[2] He was writing with the memories of World War II in Europe all too fresh in mind, and with the knowledge that the study of political history tends to concentrate on the strife and conflicts conducted between the leaders of nations. Ordinary people in their everyday lives have much more in common than do politicians: on a European scale this is well illustrated when one compares the exhibits in different folk museums, not least in my own country in Northern Ireland where the common bonds in folk life transcend the political divisions manifested so tragically in contemporary society.

In developing some of these points a selection of artifacts still in use in some parts of the British Isles and of ancient lineage will first be looked at. Next it will be shown how scholars came to realise that these objects were worthy of academic study and how, in turn, this stimulated the development of folk museums in many countries of the world.

The Past in the Present

The first example is the bannock, that round, flat loaf made from barley or oatmeal, and baked without yeast on the girdle or griddle; sometimes it is finished by toasting or 'harnin' (hardening), set on a special stand in front of the fire. The ingredients used may vary: oatmeal was the most common in nineteenth-century Ireland and Scotland; earlier it was bere, and for the well-to-do, sometimes wheat. Outside Scotland, bread made like the bannock was found in most of the countries which fringe the Atlantic shores of Europe, from Norway to the Basque country of Spain, and in a few areas of the Mediterranean. South

* A lecture given to the Open Association of the University of St. Andrews, 25th February, 1983.

65

of Scotland's border in England, and eastward in continental Europe,[3] it is replaced by leavened bread baked in the oven, a product known in Scotland only in the laird's castle. The bannock's ancestry may be prehistoric; certainly its method of baking is described in the Irish Law Tracts, recorded towards the end of the first millennium A.D;[4] and its typical artifacts – the griddle and the toasting stand, are represented on Irish sculptured crosses of the early middle ages.[5] So the humble bannock, still baked on the griddle, is a living link with the past; and with the curious inversions in taste that sometimes occur, has now a higher status than bakers' bread bought in the supermarket.

The box-bed is also so well-known as to need little description. The simplest consist of a timber-framed 'box' with enclosing curtains and a tester or roof-covering to keep the bed dry from roof-drips; the more elaborate were fine pieces of craftsmanship, with deal panelling and doors, and in Scotland some surviving examples date back to the early eighteenth century.[6] In Ireland they were placed against a back wall in the kitchen near the hearth; in Scotland they might be in a similar location, or opposite the hearth, acting as a partition between the adjoining room and the kitchen.

Box-beds provided comfort and privacy in small homes where living space was at a premium, especially if animals shared the dwelling; they accommodated parents or grandparents, and were a great comfort to the bedridden, being warm, snug and near to company. As furniture they are found in the north of Ireland, in Scotland, and from the Faroes and Norway along the North Sea coasts of Denmark and the Netherlands to Brittany.[7] Their prehistoric antecedents may be the stone-slabbed beds of the neolithic houses of Skara Brae, although it is thought these were more like settle-beds – seats by day and beds at night. They have also affinities with the wall-beds of the Hebridean black-houses of the last century,[8] and with the bed-outshot, found in Ireland north of a line from Galway to north-east Antrim. Known as the *cailleach* or *cúilleach* (back-house), this was a small projection from the back wall of the kitchen, usually built near the hearth, and roofed by a continuation of the main roof. Its history is uncertain, but similar projections are described in the Irish Law Tracts – though as food-stores rather than for beds.[9]

Piggins and noggins provide another example.

These are the small stave-built wooden vessels beautifully made from interlocked or 'feathered' staves, or held together by a thin band of ash, joined by interlocking tongues: this is a method of fastening found in Scandinavia, and further east in Asiatic Russia. These were the common vessels of the kitchen in Ireland and much of Scotland, their ancestry uncertain except that they largely replaced pottery during the first millennium A.D. One of the enigmas of our prehistory is the decline of pot-making after the late Bronze Age: nothing of similar quality was made until the wheel-turned glazed pots were sold in mediaeval towns.[10] Instead, containers made of metal or leather were used for cooking, and wood was used for plates and drinking vessels, the former being carved from the solid and the latter made as staved containers.[11]

The spade is a good example, for it is one of the most important implements in tilling the soil, its cutting edge slicing through the sod and its broad blade acting as a shovel for moving earth. In Ireland spades came in a great variety of shapes and sizes: some are like the ordinary straight-bladed implement bought in the local garden centre today, while others have narrow bent blades, quite useless for shovelling soil but perfectly adapted for under-cutting and turning the sod. In that sense this spade, found mainly in the south and west of Ireland, 'acts like a hand-plough, and the Leitrim loy is thus used in much the same way as the Scottish *cas chrom*. Once it was thought that this implement had a long ancestry, but recent work suggests it may be no older than the early eighteenth century'.[12] This leaves the ancestry of the narrow-bladed spade in doubt; but some such implement, capable of cutting the sod, must have been in use from quite early times. Sods were cut to provide roofs and walls and make fences in pre-historic times, and sods, too, were used in building the great passage-grave of Knowth.[13] The earliest plough, the so-called ard, was incapable of turning the sod, and an implement like the Irish spade must have been used to make the cultivation ridges which lie under the bogs of Mayo: they are almost identical with those still being worked in the same area today.

The sickle is another ancient implement still used occasionally in Scotland, and differing from the smooth-bladed reaping-hook in having a serrated edge with tiny, saw-like teeth. It is used differently too; a handful of grain, held in one hand, is sawn off with a backward pull, instead of the forward slashing action of the reaping-hook. The sickle is used with a gentle motion, which means it is more efficient than the hook with cereals which shed their grains easily like wheat and some varieties of barley.[14] Both implements involved backbreaking labour, usually carried out by teams of reapers, like the harvest-workers who came in their thousands from western Ireland to Scotland in the last century.

Threshing the grain after harvest involved another hand implement, the flail. It consisted of two sticks: a hand-staff, 3-4 ft. long and usually made of ash, and a shorter 'beater', made of hazel or holly. Regional variations occur in the method of joining the two parts: in one two leather caps are lashed over the ends of the sticks and a tie joined between them; in the other the tie passes through a hole in either stick or around grooves cut in each. The holed version in Ireland is confined to the north; in Scotland it is found mainly in the east and central Highlands, and on the Continent it has a sporadic distribution in Atlantic Europe. The grooved version is found in Europe in a similar area, from Scandinavia to the Pyrenees; in Ireland its distribution is mainly western, as in Scotland where it is found in the Hebrides. The capped variety, however, is more restricted in both Ireland and Scotland, mainly in Leinster and the Scottish lowlands, but it is common in much of England where it is thought to have arrived from France, ultimately from central Europe, early in mediaeval times.[15]

The final example is a type of boat once found in Scotland[16] and still used along the coasts of Connemara and Kerry in western Ireland: the *curragh*. The modern rowing curragh − sometimes used with an outboard motor − is a light boat, 25 ft. or less in length and built with tarred canvas stretched over a light 'basket-work' frame. It is immensely light and durable, powered by long narrow-bladed oars which pivot on single wooden pegs, 'thole-pins', and rowed cross-handed since the oars overlap; this method of rowing, and the use of the thole-pin, link the curragh with the Mediterranean.[17] Its form of construction is of particular interest, for boats like these were common in early Christian Ireland and Scotland: St. Columba landed from a curragh at Iona, and the one used by St. Brendan the Navigator may have reached America, as Tim Severin sought to demonstrate in his remarkable voyage across the Atlantic in 1976.[18] Vessels like these have a history extending back at least 2,000 years, and study of the modern curragh and its relation, the coracle, can tell us a great deal about the movements of early man.

The Ethnology of the Past

These 'byegones', as they were once called in museum collections, arouse interest for their own sake, for most people have at least a passing curiosity in the way their forefathers lived. But scholars have been much slower to realise that these objects of everyday life can provide clues to the past as valuable in their own way as the polished stone axe is to the expert on the neolithic or the property lease to the economic historian. We in Britain have been parti-cularly slow to recognise the potential of this field for academic study: in the 1980s only two universities in the United Kingdom promoted folklife studies through teaching departments, and this number has not increased during the past twenty years, even when university expansion was at its height.

Appropriately one was the University of Edinburgh, whose School of Scottish Studies was established with a grant from the Carnegie Trust in 1952. I say appro-priately, because it was a Secretary of the Society of Antiquaries of Scotland − a man who was also Commissioner in Lunacy for Scotland! − Dr. Arthur Mitchell, who wrote the pioneer book in the field of folklife studies: it was *The Past in the Present*, sub-titled 'What is Civilisation?', and it was the Rhind Lectures in Archaeology delivered in Edinburgh in 1876 and 1878.

I want to quote from the opening paragraph, because it expresses perfectly what Estyn Evans was to describe, many years later, as 'the emotional shock which prints in the memory the first sight of some tool or custom which has survived from an earlier culture-layer'.[19] This is precisely what happened to Arthur Mitchell:

> 'In the summer of 1864', he writes, 'I had occasion to visit Fetlar, one of the Shetland group of islands. As I walked from the landing-place to the nearest town-ship, I overtook a little boy; and while I was asking him some questions about the people and places, I observed that he was giving shape with his pocket-knife to a piece of stone. . . . I asked him what he intended to make out of the stone. 'A whorl for my mother', was the ready reply. With equal readiness he gave me the half-manufactured whorl, which I regarded as an important find'.[20]

He goes on to describe how he went home with the boy and watched the mother using the spindle, with a whorl identical to those found in prehistoric contexts. Nearly thirty years after Mitchell's final lecture had been delivered, a two-volume work was published in Ireland on a parallel theme: it was *The Elder Faiths,* subtitled 'Traces of the Elder Faiths of Ireland', by W. G. Wood-Martin. This book was also a pioneer study, seeking to demonstrate that folk-belief and custom could provide clues to the past. Its approach was more matter of fact than Sir James Frazer's *The Golden Bough,* and less literary than the works of W. B. Yeats, then hot in pursuit of the fairy hosts of Ireland, with his collaborator, Lady Gregory.

Neither of these works, nor others written about the same time, had much impact on the academics of their day. Folklife did not become a respectable field of study in Britain, and folklore was left to the amateur, though in Ireland its value in fostering a sense of national identity was recognised by the foundation of the state-sponsored Irish Folklore Commission in 1930. It might be added that Eire's then President, Dr. Douglas Hyde, had himself contributed as an academic to folklore studies.

A change in attitude was by then under way in Britain, largely as a consequence of the teaching and research of one man, H. J. Fleure, Professor of geography and anthropology at University College, Aberystwyth. Fleure was one of those giants of scholarship whose learning spans many fields: in his case, whilst trained as a zoologist, he made original contributions in four other disciplines – archaeology, anthropology, geography and history. In the present context, his major contribution was to instil in his students the awareness that an understanding of the past is essential for a comprehension of the present; and to achieve that understanding he believed folklife studies could make an important contribution, alongside the more conventional disciplines of archaeology, geography and history. Two men in particular were receptive to Fleure's ideas, and both applied his teaching in their careers. One was the late Dr. Iowerth Peate, first Curator of the Welsh Folk Museum; the other Professor Estyn Evans, first Professor of Geography at the Queen's University of Belfast and the man responsible for the foundation of the Ulster Folk Museum.

Unfortunately for Scotland, Fleure's influence did not extend north of the border – except to the Department of Geography at Dundee. Instead the development of Scotland's first folk museum depended on the enterprise of a determined individual, Isobel F. Grant, who established her own Highland Folk Museum at Kingussie in 1944. Her book *Highland Folk Ways,* published in 1961, was the first attempt to establish folklife study in Scotland on a new footing, and her success may be judged in a steady flow of subsequent publication, especially in the work of Alexander Fenton of the National Museum of Antiquities of Scotland. His many books and articles include a definitive work, *Scottish Country Life,* published in 1976.

Preserving the Past

So far Scotland does not have a National Folk Museum, unlike Wales or the provincial institution in Ulster: does it need one? To answer this we need to ask first what folk museums seek to do, and I will illustrate this with reference to several examples from different countries. Arthur Hazelius, the Swedish scholar who originated the idea of the folk museum, saw it as an institution which portrayed the cultural history of a community, thereby fostering a sense of identity and understanding of its past.[21] It achieves this by recreating the cultural setting of daily life in the homes, farmyards and craft shops, the streets and even the fields of ordinary people over several centuries. Hence the museum is based not on showcase displays in conventional galleries, but in real buildings, brought from their original locations and recreated in the museum's grounds.

Skansen in Stockholm is the first and greatest of these museums, the Frilandsmuseum near Copenhagen and at Arnhem in the Netherlands are others, developed about the same period and following a similar pattern. In the United Kingdom, the Welsh Folk Museum at St. Fagans, established in 1946, and the Ulster Folk Museum at Cultra Manor near Belfast, founded in 1959, are both closely modelled on the Scandinavian prototypes. Both are major institutions in their own right, with research staffs who have fostered the scholarship which one normally expects to be provided within universities. Unfortunately neither institution has a close link with the nearby universities in Cardiff and Belfast respectively, and folklife studies lack the stimulus and mental discipline provided through university teaching at undergraduate and postgraduate level.

Curiously the universities where folklife studies are taught have no folk museums associated with them. Edinburgh has its largely postgraduate School of Scottish Studies, Leeds its Department of Folklife and Dialect Studies, and University College, Dublin absorbed the former state-financed Irish Folklore Commission some years ago to become the Department of Irish Folklore. The absence of a national folk museum in the Republic of Ireland is unfortunate, and surprising in view of the long-established support provided by government for the folklore archive. In fact the Republic's first folk museum at Bunratty, near Limerick, is a by-product of its tourist industry. Someone with an eye to business saw the potential of creating a folk village beside a fifteenth century castle already used for staging 'mediaeval banquets' for tourists, and Bunratty Folk Park opened in 1964, its first exhibit a farmhouse threatened with demolition by the extension of a runway at the nearby Shannon International Airport. Purists may regard Bunratty with some disfavour since many of its buildings are copies rather than genuine dwellings; and 'the park' is orientated specifically towards the tourist. But I believe this type of development does provide an important function: tourists do show a genuine interest in traditional popular culture, and imaginative exhibits such as Bunratty fulfil this need. It is an approach pioneered in the U.S.A., at places such as Williamsburg, and adapted here in slightly different form.

There is one further type of museum, first developed in Britain at Cregneash in the Isle of Man, and followed here in Scotland at Auchindrain near Inveraray in Argyll. This is the presentation of houses in their original setting – instead of transferring selected examples to the more artificial setting of a Folk Museum. An architectural historian has referred to folk museums, aptly but unkindly, as 'architectural zoos', where threatened homes may be protected. Preservation on site raises formidable problems of organisation and finance, but such developments are of immense importance since they preserve that past for the present within its own environment and among the descendants of its own people. Both Cregneash and Auchindrain are important projects, and it is to be hoped that the farsightedness of Marion Campbell of Kilberry and the hard work of those who have supported the Museum of Argyll Farming Life, since 1962, will be backed by the finance necessary to ensure the survival of Auchindrain as a unique example of a farming township.

But Auchindrain is no substitute for a national folk museum, nor is it intended to be so. A folk museum, in the words of Trefor Owen, Curator of the Welsh Folk Museum, should be 'a cultural centre of the nation which it serves'. Northern Ireland has a people deeply divided by religious affiliation and political aspiration – yet its folklife, as portrayed in its folk museum, shows that the shared culture of the past runs much deeper than the divisions of the present. Scotland is not like Ulster, but it too has its divisions: between highland and lowland, east and west, Glasgow and Edinburgh. A national folk museum could portray these regional varieties within the context of a common culture that is Scottish, and which is very different from the clans and tartans, the kings and the claymores which symbolise Scotland to those who follow the country's tourist literature.

References

1. Thomas, C., 'Archaeology and Folk-life Studies', in *Gwerin* 3 (1960), 8.
2. Erixon, S., 'Some points of view with regard to International Cartographic Activities', in *Laos* 3 (1955), 63.
3. Evans, E. E., *Irish Folk Ways*, London 1957, 77.
4. Lucas, A. T., 'Irish Food before the Potato', in *Gwerin* 3 (1960), 10.
5. Evans, E. E., *op. cit.*, 79.
6. Grant, I. F., *Highland Folk Ways*, London, 1961, 168-70.
7. Evans, E. E., *op. cit.*, 86.
8. Mitchell, A., *The Past in the Present*, Edinburgh, 1880, 50.
9. Lucas, A. T., 'Contributions to the history of the Irish house: a possible ancestry of the Bed outshot', in *Folk Life* 8 (1970), 96.
10. Evans, E. E., *op. cit.*, 73-5; Grant, I. F., *op. cit.*, 178.
11. Evans, E. E., *op. cit.*, 133.
12. Gailey, A. and Fenton, A., *The Spade*, Belfast, 1970, 46.
13. *Ibid.*, 5.
14. Fenton, A., *Scottish Country Life*, Edinburgh, 1976, 52-6; Evans, E. E., *op. cit.*, 129-30; Payne, F. G., 'The retention of simple agricultural techniques', in *Gwerin* 3 (1959), 129-30.
15. Evans, E. E., *op. cit.*, 213; Grant, I. F., *op. cit.*, 113; Fenton, A., 'Hand Threshing in Scotland', in *Acta Ethnographica* 29, 3-4 (1980), 349-389.
16. Fenton, A., 'The Currach in Scotland', in *Scottish Studies* 16 (1972).
17. Evans, E. E., *op. cit.*, 233-40.
18. Severin, T., *The Brendon Voyage*, London, 1978.
19. Evans, E. E., *op. cit.*, xiii.
20. Mitchell, A., *op. cit.*
21. Thompson, G. B., in Gailey, A., and D. Ò hÒgain, edd., *Gold under the Furze*, Dublin, 1982, 44.

Scottish Agricultural Improvement Societies, 1723-1835

R C Boud

Until recently, the writings concerned with agrarian change in the eighteenth and nineteenth centuries paid little attention to the means by which agricultural knowledge was diffused. Macdonald,[1] in turning from the theoretical notion of the landlord as the source of agricultural information, has questioned the practical aspects of how Northumberland farmers acquired knowledge of the new agricultural techniques of the period and, drawing evidence from county sources, has cited influences such as newspapers, agricultural societies, geographical movement of farmers and tenants, agricultural apprenticeships and correspondence.

Recent studies by Hudson[2], Fox[3] and Goddard[4,5] have been concerned in particular with the role of agricultural societies as part of this dissemination process. Hudson's study has tended to focus attention on the role of the larger societies such as the Bath and West, and the Dublin Society. That of Fox has described the growth in England of local farmers' associations, and Goddard's the role of agricultural societies in England and Wales and, specifically, the activities of the Royal Agricultural Society of England. As yet, no assessment has been made of early Scottish agricultural associations, and this paper seeks to describe their development and role in Scotland during the period 1723-1835.

I. Early Scottish agricultural societies

Modern writers such as Handley,[6] Symon[7] and Bedford Franklin,[8] when recording the general progress of Scottish agriculture during the eighteenth and nineteenth centuries, have all mentioned, in varying degrees of depth, the institution and demise of the three early Edinburgh societies that were to influence the initial development of Scottish husbandry: the Society of Improvers (founded 1723), the Select Society (founded 1754) and the Edinburgh Society (founded 1755). Similarly, these writers have

described the subsequent establishment in 1784 of the Highland Society (later to be known as the Highland and Agricultural Society) and its role in the advancement of farming in Scotland. In addition to the general treatment afforded these four Edinburgh societies, certain writers – for example Ramsay,[9] McCallum,[10] Smith[11] and Emerson[12] – have compiled accounts of specific institutions concerned with agriculture.

However, little concerted attention has been paid to the various smaller and less prestigious local agricultural societies that were established in many areas of Scotland in the hundred or so years that followed the formation in 1723 of the Society of Improvers, the first Scottish agricultural society. In modern accounts of agricultural history, writers have tended to intersperse examples of the activities of agricultural societies amongst their texts, more as scattered illustrations to their general theme, rather than develop the topic in its own right. In view of the paucity of both books and articles pertaining to such organisations in Scotland, it is of interest to ask a number of basic questions regarding these societies. For example, how many Scottish societies were formed and what was their distribution pattern over the country? Which social groups comprised their membership, and to what activities did this membership devote its energies? However, often the active lives of such organisations were brief, and their records are now lost, if indeed records were kept. Therefore, in attempting to piece together aspects of the agricultural society movement, one is often forced to use both sparse and scattered sources.

In what appears to be the earliest published list of agricultural societies, Arthur Young in 1803[13] noted five Scottish associations.[14] In another, published by the Bath and West of England Society seven years later,[15] twenty named societies were located in Scotland. Although this latter list carries no details of

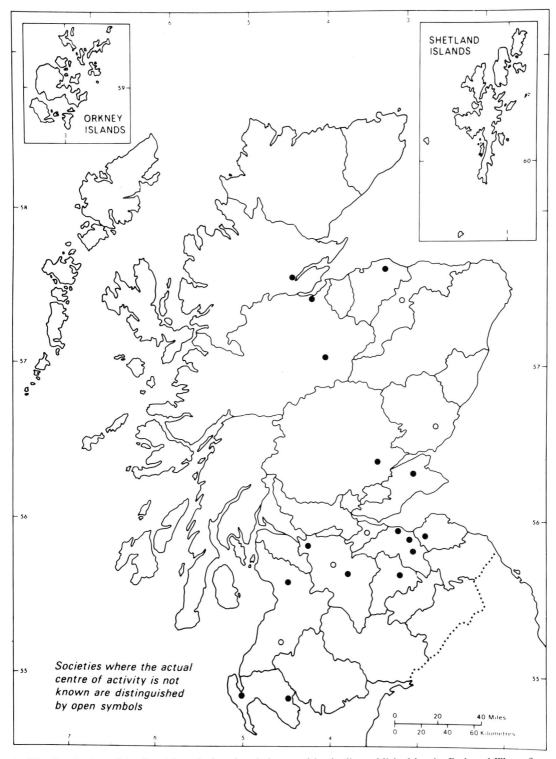

1. The distribution of the Scottish agricultural societies noted in the list published by the Bath and West of England Society in 1810.

authorship, references found elsewhere in the journal show that the information was collected 'under the direction of the Society'[16] by its Secretary, Robert Ricards. Mention is also made that the list had been 'distributed in another form through many parts of the united kingdom'. Unfortunately, no further reference is made to this isolated but interesting comment. As to the form in which the list was distributed, the method of its distribution, under whose auspices, and for what purpose, we are left frustratingly unaware. However, from the journal's preface one can sense a little of the atmosphere that prevailed in the science of agriculture at this time and which, in all probability, promoted the compilation of such a list. It was a subject that was 'happily rising in estimation among all ranks of people' and had thus 'become of more importance than ever'.[17] The Society flattered itself that through its own example it had nurtured the prevailing spirit of emulation and contributed to the 'great and growing increase' of agricultural societies.

When plotted on a map (Fig. 1), four-fifths of the Scottish societies listed by the Bath and West of England Society are located in a broad arc from Wigtownshire in the west, through the Lothians, to Angus in the east, the remainder being situated in the Moray Firth area. Although it is not possible to state with any degree of certainty how many Scottish societies actually existed at the time Ricards compiled his list, doubts must be expressed regarding its comprehensiveness. For example, the absence of societies in the Aberdeenshire area is contrary to trends to which I draw attention later in this paper.

The establishment of the agricultural improvement societies that were greatly to influence Scottish farming practices commenced during the first half of the eighteenth century, with the formation at Edinburgh in 1723 of 'The Honourable the Society of Improvers in the Knowledge of Agriculture in Scotland', the earliest European agricultural society. The claim by the society's secretary, Robert Maxwell, that its membership was made up of 'three hundred and upwards of the greatest, wisest, and most learned of a Nation'[18] appears to border on the extravagant. However, the society undoubtedly enjoyed a distinguished membership, of which over a third were dukes, peers and knights, and also included Senators of the College of Justice, Writers to the Signet, advocates, Barons of the Court of Exchequer, doctors,

army officers and university professors.[19]

As a forerunner of all British agricultural societies, the Society of Improvers was faced with perhaps the most difficult of evangelising tasks. One aspect of the influence of this early society may be gauged from the variety of questions concerning agricultural improvement that were addressed to the society 'from every corner of the country'. Both the initial questions and the Society's answers were published in 1743 by Maxwell in *Select Transactions* . . . .[20] In addition to acting as a 'clearing house' for the variety of agricultural problems encountered by its members, the Society had displayed early enterprise in publishing an agricultural treatise in 1724.[21]

With the exception of both the Hebrides and the Highland region north of Perthshire, those who comprised the society's non-titled membership were to be found in almost every county. Spread throughout the Lowland area, the greatest membership concentrations were in the Lothians, Fife, South-east Perthshire and Aberdeenshire, before thinning out in the coastal area south of the Moray Firth. No doubt it was this geographical influence that prompted Maxwell to write: 'Before this Society commenced, we seemed to have been Centuries behind our Neighbours of England; now I hope we are within less than one'.[22]

Following the deaths of its founder-members, the Society lost some of its early impetus, and was disbanded about the time of the 1745 Rebellion. However, the creation of the Society of Improvers had paved the way for the establishment of other local agricultural societies, Maxwell giving stimulus to the idea through the medium of *Select Transactions* . . . (1743) by posing the question, 'if there was a Society set up in every County, how much would the Spirit of Husbandry be raised and diffused?'[23]

The conception of the establishment of a network of smaller societies throughout Scotland devoted to the advancement of agriculture was no doubt part-Utopian to Maxwell. By the time that Maxwell had published the idea in 1743, a society had already been established in each of the Buchan and East Lothian areas, and prior to 1784, the year in which the Highland Society was established, a gradual but significant increase in the number of established societies can be traced. For reasons that will be discussed later, many of these societies were of only short duration and their activities are seldom well documented. Thus, one cannot hope to present a full résumé of their histories. My research has shown that *at least* fourteen such societies with known establishment dates were formed in the sixty years from 1723 to 1784. However, this total cannot be considered comprehensive, firstly, because of limited extant information and, secondly, because of self-imposed limitations. For example, only those societies are included for which definitie institution dates have been ascertained. When plotted on a base-map (Fig. 2), their geographical locations give emphasis to the fact that, in this period, areas of agricultural advance were centred on both the Aberdeenshire and Lothian regions. Additionally, the distribution of these societies suggests that the agricultural influence of the Society of Improvers in the Lothians was in part paralleled by that of the Buchan society ·in the Aberdeenshire area.

This latter organisation, 'A Small Society of Farmers in Buchan', was formed about 1730 and had a membership, drawn mainly from the counties of Aberdeenshire and Banffshire, which included such eminent persons as Alexander Lord Pitsligo, the Hon. Alexander Fraser of Strichen, Sir James Elphinstone of Logie, Alexander Garden of Troup and George Skene of Skene.[24] The society was sufficiently well established five years after its formation to publish a book[25] which, later, was included as an appendix in the Board of Agriculture's report on Banff (1812).[26] Because most agricultural books assumed the possession of a clay soil and 'quite overlookt' their own hazely ('sand and light earth') type of soil, the society published the work out of 'concern for the common good of their country'.[27] The membership's realisation of the value of documenting practical farming expertise is clearly indicated in the preface to the work which informs the reader that it contains 'nothing purely speculative, but a plain and genuine relation of our practice, as we have learned from tradition, and our own repeated experience, put into method, to ease our memories and for the instruction of beginners'.[28] That a ready market existed amongst the affluent for such a book may be assumed from the fact that sixteen subscribers each took ten copies.

The 'traditional' viewpoint regarding the backward state of Scottish agriculture and the rate and degree of agricultural change during the late eighteenth and early nineteenth centuries has tended to emanate from sources such as the Old Statistical Account

(1791-9) and the Board of Agriculture Reports (1793-1816), as well as the writings of individual improvers. Stemming from Caird's early argument that 'Scotland's rural landscape is in fact a landscape of "revolution" rather than one of slow evolution',[29] Whittington's search for a new evaluation of Scottish improvement has included the questioning of the propriety of the continued use of the term 'Agricultural Revolution'[30] and has drawn responses from Mills,[31] Parry,[32] Adams[33] and Whyte.[34] Comparisons between English and Scottish agriculture have been made when either supporting or challenging Whittington's paper, and in the context of this study it is of interest to compare the early growth of the farming association movement in Scotland with that of England.

Examination of the Board of Agriculture Reports of English counties shows that most included a section concerned with the activities of agricultural societies. Few recorded more than two farming associations in the county on which they were reporting, whilst five commented that no such societies existed. The associations that are noted were formed mainly in the period 1783-1801. As noted by Fox, these figures cannot be considered comprehensive.[35] Nevertheless, they help to bring to light trends of value. For example, the present study shows that at least eleven Scottish societies had been established before the formation of the two earliest societies (1772-1773) noted in the Board of Agriculture Reports of English counties.[36] This early growth of agricultural societies in the progressive areas of Scotland is indicative of a diffusion movement that, surprisingly, was in advance of that in England.

It may be regarded also as a trend that can be viewed against the recent contributions by both historians and geographers on the processes of change in the Scottish rural landscape.[37] Concerned with the role of people as agents of agricultural change, one of these studies has suggested that agricultural societies represent a secondary diffusion rather than a primary, because the societies were formed 'only when interest had been roused'.[38] When this point, which I find acceptable, is considered in conjunction with the above evidence of an early Scottish agricultural society movement, further weight is given to the views espoused by Smout and Fenton,[39] Whittington[40] and Whyte[41, 42] of the existence of a slowly accelerating Scottish agricultural development in the seventeenth

F

1 The Honourable the Society of Improvers
2 A Small Society of Farmers in Buchan
3 Ormiston Society
4 Society for Improving of Agriculture and Manufactures in the Shire of Ayr
5 A Society of Honest Farmers residing in the Counties of Banff and Aberdeen
6 Edinburgh Society for Encouraging Arts, Sciences, Manufactures and Agriculture
7 Glenmuick Farming Society
8 The Farming Club at Gordon's Mill
9 Dalkeith Farmers' Society
10 An Aberdeen Society for the Encouragement of Agricultural Arts and Manufactures
11 Kilbarchan and Neighbourhood Agricultural Society
12 The Society for the Encouragement of Agriculture within the Counties of Dumfries and Wigton and Stewartry of Kirkcudbright
13 The Highland Society
14 Buchan Farmers' Society

Societies where the actual centre of activity is not known are distinguished by open symbols

SHETLAND ISLANDS

Agricultural Societies 1723–84

2. The distribution of Scottish agricultural societies having known establishment dates, 1723-84.

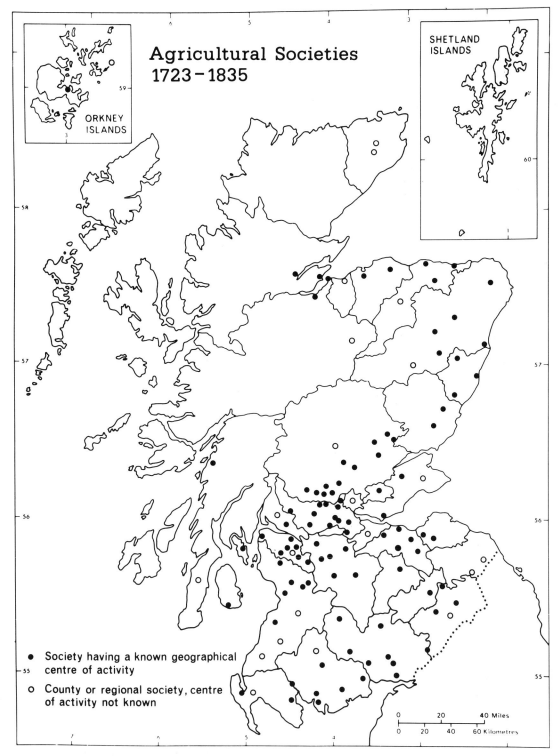

3. The distribution of traced Scottish agricultural societies, 1723-1834. The societies plotted on the map are those listed in Table 1.

and early eighteenth centuries which formed a prelude to the orthodox 'agricultural revolution'. It is true that the evidence of early societies tends to be drawn from what now is often considered to be suspect, late eighteenth century literature; however, it is not likely that references to the *existence* of such societies were the product of either exaggeration or imagination.

II. *The distribution of the societies*

Reference has already been made to the brevity of the active lives of many of the organisations. The society that was established in 1776 with the intention of improving agriculture in Dumfriesshire and Kirkcudbrightshire and which 'only lasted for a few years'[43] was far from being exceptional. The ephemeral nature of many of the societies can be judged from the experiences of David Souter, the writer of the Banff agricultural report who, when writing of the establishment of 'A small Society of farmers in Buchan', claimed not to have 'fallen in with an individual who has even so much as heard of the existence of this society',[44] a comment that was made a mere seventy years after the event. In the light of this remark, it is not surprising that it has been found possible to ascertain both the establishment and disbandment dates of only a small proportion of the 133 societies whose existence I have traced and which are listed in Table 1. The geographical distribution of these societies (Fig. 3) shows that, during the period under review, the greatest concentration of societies was to be found within the area bounded in the north by a line drawn from Garelochead to Montrose, and in the south by one extending from Ayr to Eyemouth. Although this survey cannot be considered exhaustive, in all probability it is a sufficiently quantitative generalisation to support this discussion.

Table 1. Scottish Agricultural Societies, 1723-1835

Map No.	Agricultural Society
41	Aberdeen Society for the Encouragement of Agriculture, Arts and Manufactures
57	Alford society
124	Annandale Agricultural Society
125	Annandale Farmers' Society
123	Annandale Society for Promoting Improvements
126	Annandale, Upper, Agricultural Society
92	Ardoch Agricultural Society
122	Association for the Improvement of Agriculture
144	Avondale Farmers' Society

Map No.	Agricultural Society
70	Ayr County Association
62	Ayr, Society for improving of Agriculture and Manufactures in the Shire of
78	Badenoch and Strathspey Society
110	Banff and Aberdeen, A Society of Honest Farmer, residing in
12	Banffshire Farmer Club
13	Banffshire Farming Society
68	Beith Farmers' Club
75	Black Isle Farming Society
24	Blairgowrie society
72	Border Agricultural Society
14	Buchan, a Small Society of Farmers in
3	Bute Farmers' Society
102	Bute Farmer' Society
28	Caithness Agricultural Society
27	Caithness society
143	Calder-water-head Agricultural Society
67	Carrick Farmers' Club
65	Clackmannanshire agricultural club
112	Clydesdale agricultural society
31	Collessie Agricultural Society
37	Corresponding and Improving Society of Farmers (Glasgow)
20	Coupar Angus society
26	Crieff Society
66	Dalkeith Farmers' Society
18	Deeside Agricultural Association
82	Denny farmers' club
93	Doune Farmers' Club
38	Dumbartonshire Agricultural Society
22	Dunblane Farming Society
81	Dunipace farmers' society
129	Dunscore farmers' society
148	Eaglesham Farmers' Society
145	East Kilbride, Farmer's Society of
113	Eddlestone agricultural society
63	Edinburgh Society for Encouraging Arts, Sciences, Manufactures and Agriculture (The Select Society)
11	Elgin Farming Club
85	Endrick Agricultural Society
46	Erskine, Inchinnan and Renfrew farming club
105	Eskdale and Liddesdale Farmers' Association
16	Fettercairn Club
32	Fife Farming Society
19	Forfarshire (Eastern) Farming Association
10	Forres Farming Club
77	Fort George Agricultural Society
71	Galloway, New, Agricultural Society
71A	Galloway, New, Farming Society

Note

By capitalisation, distinction has been made in this list between

    (a) societies, the exact name of which has been ascertained, e.g. Collessie Agricultural Society

and (b) societies, the exact name of which it has not been possible to ascertain, e.g. Clydesdale agricultural society.

Whilst the improving society movement arose in great part from the national fervour for agricultural advance, it also stemmed from the promptings of key centres of stimulus such as the prestigious Bath and West of England and Highland societies. Although in 1810 the former society was of the opinion that its own example had contributed to the proliferation of local societies, such influence would have affected in the main only English agriculture, and one must ask which were the main agencies that gave stimulus to the establishment of a plethora of agricultural clubs in Scotland. As early as 1794 the worth of farming clubs was sufficiently apparent to the agricultural writer, James Robertson, for him to suggest that the Board of Agriculture, which had been established in August of the previous year, should give its encouragement to the establishment of corresponding societies in each district or county. Robertson further advocated that half the membership should consist of heritors and the remainder of tenants,[45] and also that the substance of their Quarterly Meeting discussions should be conveyed annually to the Board. Although nothing of such a formal nature was attempted on a nationwide basis, the Board's establishment gave stimulus to the movement, and 'above fifty societies . . . were soon formed'.[46]

Ten years after the latter comment was published, recognition was given in the pages of the New Statistical Account[47] to another important influence – that of the Highland Society. In 1792, eight years after its foundation, the General Meeting of the Society had given approval to a report, submitted at the request of its Directors, by Macleod Bannatyne of Kaims. The report recommended to

> gentlemen of the country at large, and particularly such as are members of this Society, to form local and corresponding societies for the improvement of the particular counties and districts within which they may be established, as a measure likely to be of much advantage, both from the separate exertions of such societies, and as the means of promoting the views of this Institution.[48]

This recommendation was pursued with diligence by the society, and contacts were made with the more prestigious agricultural institutions such as the Board of Agriculture, the Society of Arts, the Bath and West of England Agricultural Society, and the Dublin Society and Farming Society of Ireland, as well as with 'many of the local agricultural societies of Scotland'.[49] Of all the Highland Society's exertions on behalf of Scottish agriculture, the New Statistical Account writer considered 'the formation of local Associations throughout the country' perhaps to have been the most important.[50]

It is not necessary here to discuss the degree of encouragement afforded by the Board of Agriculture and the Highland Society. Nevertheless, it is pertinent to note a significant rise in Scottish societies during the next fifteen or so years. Evidence has been found to show that the total of fourteen societies, having known establishment dates, noted earlier as having been formed prior to the formation of the Highland Society, by 1800 had risen to forty-one.

III. *Membership of the societies*

Many agricultural societies relied on a membership gained from several adjacent parishes, others recruited their members on a district or county basis whilst, in spite of its regional name, the Highland Society's membership must be considered as national.

Fox has classified four different levels of farming associations: 'County', 'Provincial', 'District' and 'Farmers' Clubs'.[51] Whilst the first three descriptions are self-explanatory, the last requires comment. Both Fox and Goddard have noted a social, as well as a size, distinction between the generally larger 'agricultural societies' and the generally smaller 'farmers' clubs'. Although the former author has noted a slight difference in the emphasis of activities between the two types of associations, any difference was 'of degree rather than of kind';[52] Goddard has argued, however, that the clubs 'served particularly to advance the cause of the tenant farmer'.[53] It is true that of the associations established in Scotland prior to 1784 (Fig. 2), a time at which the membership consisted mainly of wealthy landowners, only one of the fourteen societies (the Gordon's Mill) termed itself a club. However, no Scottish evidence has been found to give definite support to Goddard's argument and, thus, the views of Fox would appear to be more correct with regard to Scottish associations.

From the above discussion of the territorial aspects of the associations, it can be seen that the size of the membership would have varied enormously: by agreement, the Gordon's Mill Farming Club's did not exceed 15,[54] whilst that of the Middleton Farming Society's was limited to 30.[55] By contrast, six years after its formation in 1784, the membership of the Fife Farming Society had risen to nearly 200,[56] and that of the Highland Society in 1821 was 1212.[57]

When reviewing the influence of the Buchan society, the writer of the Board of Agriculture report on Banff comments that, in all probability, one of the achievements of the association had been to direct the attention of noblemen and gentlemen to the general condition of agriculture which 'it is well known, had been accounted much below the notice of people of fashion'.[58] That there had been a marked change of attitude towards the science within this particular social group can be seen from the membership of the early improvement societies. Although precise details of the membership of many of the societies have not survived, a broad impression of the social status of the membership can be gleaned from the scattered observations found amongst contemporary publications and documents.

Associations such as the Society of Improvers and the Edinburgh Society were formed from men of wealth and education, and the membership of the early local organisations tended to be similar in constitution. Just as the Buchan society was composed almost wholly of proprietors,[59] it was a group of Aberdeenshire noblemen and gentlemen who in 1760 formed a society for the improvement of agriculture, arts and manufactures, and who were later joined by others of similar status from the counties of Banff and Mearns.[60] Not all sections of the landed class, however, were improvers or innovators, and regret was sometimes expressed that there were those who did not share the enthusiasm for experiment and change in the traditional system of husbandry. The transactions of the society formed to encourage agriculture in the counties of Dumfries, Wigton and Kirkcudbright noted in 1776 that its subscription list was 'still wanting, the names of many Gentlemen of property within the three Counties'.[61] As noted above, the membership of the Society of Improvers, a national society, also included a number of professional men. However, even the Gordon's Mill Farming Club, a smaller society, could count amongst its members the Principal and several professors of King's College, Aberdeen,[62] although it is likely that at this time the infiltration of farming by the professional classes was only just beginning.

To find the reasons for the preponderance of wealthy landowners in the membership of the early societies, one must turn to the elements of change that were permeating the agriculture of the day. This improving atmosphere, 'heavy' in some areas and 'thin' in others, was engendered by innovations that were advocated in the light of experiments conducted by individuals. This sifting of the 'practical wheat' from the 'impractical chaff' was a necessary exercise which, to have validity, could be carried out only by diligent testing in a number of Scottish areas having a wide variety of soils and climatic conditions. However, such trials, even if successful, could be deemed suitable only for the particular geographical area in which the trials took place. Additionally, those who were sufficiently flexible to put on one side the traditional practices of the past and consider the new agricultural ideas were often handicapped by lack of knowledge, finance or facilities. These problems could be further complicated by fluctuations in seasonal weather patterns, so that the successful crop of one year could become the failure of the next. That a reasoned appraisal of experiments could be ascertained only over a number of years presented the farming community with, in the words of Arthur Young, 'a scene of difficulty found in no other art'[63] and, because of such complications, many innovative farmers desiring to introduce the new agricultural methods were precluded from taking part in the great 'Improving' movement. Basically, it was those individuals who had the opportunity to experiment over a period of time, as well as the finances to absorb financial loss if the experiments or innovations failed, i.e. the members of the wealthy land owner class, who could consider participation in innovative, long-term experimentation with reasonable hopes of success.

In contrast to the general trend of the membership of agricultural societies being formed predominantly by the landowner class, a few farsighted individuals had realised that agricultural improvement had also to take place amongst those who formed the lower part of the farming pyramid. For example, as early as 1756 Captain Mackenzie of Dalmoir had formed a farming society amongst his own tenants in the Culblaine area, to which 'any man of a good moral character'[64] was admitted. Additionally a later society, the Gargunnock Farmer Club of Stirlingshire, when founded in 1796, besides promoting agricultural improvements, also aimed to bring together landlord and tenant and thus arrest the tendency for social intercourse to be confined to 'ceremonious visits between persons of similar fortune and rank'.[65]

Although the paternalistic views to be found in both Mackenzie's society and that at Gargunnock were not typical of agricultural societies of the day, it is of interest that by 1810 George Dempster of Dunnichen, a politician and member of the earlier mentioned Select Society,[66] was able to comment without reservation that such institutions 'brought pleasantly together landlord and tenant, and enabled them to be mutually helpful'.[67] It is likely that the comments of this respected agriculturalist, whose farming knowledge of Forfarshire had been recognised by Sir John Sinclair[68] and who in 1803 had founded the Lunan and Vinney Water Farming Society,[69] reflect the changes which were taking place in the social mix of the membership of many of the societies at this time. Although it is pertinent to consider such topics as the predominant social groups which made up the membership of such societies, it should not be forgotten that the principal contribution of the early organisations was that they brought together those having common agricultural interests, even though of the same class, and that this provided the opportunities for the discussion of farming problems as well as the sharing of observations and experiences. Later, this role was to develop in importance as societies provided common ground on which members of *differing* social backgrounds could meet together.

A decisive influence in limiting the membership of many early societies to the more affluent strata of society would have been the high cost of the annual subscriptions. It is probable that some societies set a high figure deliberately in order that the society should remain exclusive. For example, the exclusiveness of the Moray Farmer Club, instituted in 1798, is revealed by its rules, which were first published in 1821. On being admitted to the society, each new member was required to pay the Secretary five guineas entrance money and the current year's subscription. This latter charge amounted to £1-8-0, of which eighteen shillings was payment for nine club dinners, ten shillings being for the general purpose fund of the Society.[70] As a ploughman's wage towards the end of the eighteenth century was between five and seven pounds per annum,[71] it can be seen that such a financial commitment could be just as much of a hurdle to aspiring members as the social restrictions of the period. In contrast, the Stronsay, Orkney society's bye-laws reveal an enterprising and democratic attitude towards the subscriptions of its membership which were ranked in four different classes according to the areal extent of the farms they possessed. These circumstances, therefore, had brought about the formation of a society to which

'almost all the farmers in the island'[72] belonged and where the smaller farmer was not excluded by a high subscription charge, and thus could learn from the experiences of those possessing larger estates. Some societies related the size of their subscriptions to the particular range of services offered to the membership. The annual contribution of members of the Fettercairn Club, Kincardineshire was fixed at a level that would allow for both the provision of prizes for its agricultural competitions and the maintenance of a club library.[73]

IV. *Activities of the societies*

Nothing is so beneficial to the farmer as the opportunity of comparing his stock with others, a feeling subscribed to by George Rennie, the East Lothian improver, who would comment that he never went twenty miles from home but he came back with a red face.[74] From the recognition of farming deficiencies was engendered the spirit of agricultural emulation, a feeling further heightened by a healthy sense of rivalry. Such factors provided fertile ground for the local activities of the societies. Undoubtedly, a great many of the societies imparted agricultural knowledge and experiences by way of formal discussion. The regulations of the Bute Farmers' Society include the rule that, 'At each meeting a subject relative to agriculture or the breeding of stock will be appointed for discussion at next meeting, when any member may state his observations and the Preses will sum up the sense of the meeting, which will be inserted in the Minute-Book'.[75] The rules of the Middleton Farming Society 'expected (my emphasis) that members will come prepared, either with a written essay, or to speak at large on the subject'.[76] However, it is too simplistic merely to group the activities of these local societies under an umbrella phrase of 'discussion of agricultural matters'. Although the importance of such an activity in the diffusion of agricultural knowledge need not be emphasised, it is likely that many of the less articulate members would have quickly tired of such a diet.

Examination of the records of many of the societies shows that whilst agrarian discussion formed an important part of their programmes, the topic was far from being the sole item. Most societies gave strong encouragement to the improvement of the practical aspects of agriculture. The fusion of practical farming and local rivalry provided the stimulus for members to compete for premiums of medals or money awarded for excellence in the art of ploughing. Annual matches, at which medals or cash premiums were awarded to the best performers, were staged which improved standards of ploughing and, additionally, proved popular local events. First held at Alloa in 1784[77] at the suggestion of Hugh Reoch, a tenant of J. F. Erskine, later the Earl of Mar, ploughing matches soon spread to many other parts of Scotland. That such competitions excited local interest and provided the opportunity for the farming fraternity to meet together may be adjudged by the *Greenock Advertiser's* account of the second annual ploughing match arranged by the Greenock and Inverkip Farmer and Agricultural Society in 1803. On this occasion, eleven ploughs competed 'in the presence of the Judges and upwards of 1,000 spectators'.[78] The Gargunnock Farmer Club claimed that by such competitive means 'the mode of ploughing within the club . . . improved beyond its own sanguine expectation',[79] although reservations were expressed in some quarters that such competitions at times fostered 'a propensity to vanity and idleness'[80] in successful ploughmen who, at times, became 'insolent and extravagant in their demands of wages'.[81] The considerable emphasis on ploughing during this period may be gauged from the fact that, far from its being merely one facet in the farming club programme, some agricultural societies such as the Renfrewshire owed their origins to an earlier ploughing-club parent.[82]

When comparing the activities of societies, both large and small, it is tempting to underestimate the impact of the latter. Such an attitude could be mistaken. For, to use the generalisation of Lord Brougham, 'Great Institutions do not so forcibly indicate the universal eagerness for knowledge as those upon a minor scale, and established in small districts'.[83] The worth of the smaller societies in agricultural improvement stemmed mainly from a *local* membership of like-minded individuals having the freedom to mould the activities of their club to suit their own particular interests. Often, these interests sprang from the agricultural characteristics of the geographical areas in which the associations were situated. For example, the attention of many societies focused on the improvement of livestock. In an effort to improve the breed of draught horses in their area, members of the Garioch Club purchased in

1811 a stallion for shared use, each subscriber to the scheme being allowed to have three mares served annually at a cost of one guinea for each mare.[84] Periodic stock shows were arranged at which cash and medal prizes were awarded for cattle, horses, sheep and swine. The competitive aspects of such shows provided incentives to the exhibitors, recognition to local breeds of animals and, by careful judging, the establishment of characteristics and standards for various stock. Not surprisingly, the verdicts of the judges did not always meet with universal approval, although the dissension shown at some of the awards made at the cattle show of the Farmer's Club of the Middle Ward of Lanarkshire was fortunately rare. There, the matter developed into a local scandal. The prevalent want of confidence in the management of the show was demonstrated over a period of a year in the columns of the *Clydesdale Journal*. Accusations of chicanery were made against the judges, such views appearing in the newspaper together with the expressed belief that if a certain exhibitor would send to the show 'a Cow without the head, or an udder, she would be sure of the prize'.[85]

At the stock shows, awards were also offered for such diverse, but nevertheless important, aspects of farming as cheese and butter[86] and farming implements, etc.[87] However, not all aspects of farming improvement for which premiums were offered could be judged at the local agricultural show, and the judging of competitions for areas of drained land[88] and the cleanliness of farms[89] had to be carried out *in situ*.

With the exception of the county organisations, most societies drew their membership from the parish which they served, although a few clubs benefited from corresponding with agriculturalists in other areas. The articles and regulations of the Improving Renfrewshire Farmers, dated 1788, noted the advantages that might be gained from 'corresponding with persons and societies . . . in different places of the country at large, where agriculture is brought to the greatest perfection'.[90] Another such society, that at Culblaine, was 'greatly advantaged' by correspondence with members in Edinburgh, Aberdeen and Forres by whom they were persuaded to give trials to new varieties of seeds such as lint and flax.[91] Although there were 'no great expectations within the County', the raising of flax allowed some of the Culblaine society to 'declare that they have cleared their rent this same year'.[92] The value of good quality seeds, purchased from the society's funds, was recognised by the Banffshire Farming Society, and considered to be of sufficient importance to be written into the rules when drafted in 1785.[93]

In an effort to set standards of good husbandry, the Strathallan Farmers Club, soon after its institution in 1804, commenced the practice of agricultural self-analysis.[94] A committee was appointed with a view to making a thorough inspection of the farms of individual members and compiling a report on the working of the land as well as crop prospects. Fastidiously, the committee compiled reports of great length in which were to be found many critical references to the prevalence of weeds such as sorrel, nettles, etc. However, as such a self-critical approach to the improvement of husbandry required both honesty from the inspecting committee and tolerance from those being reported upon, it was an exercise that gained few adherents in other societies.

In addition to learning about, and experimenting with, the new agricultural ideas, the farming fraternity began to appreciate that through membership of a properly organised farming society it enjoyed a greater degree of influence, and that when working in concert they could bring about agricultural improvements which to the individual farmer would have been merely Utopian. For example, prior to 1778 there had been no regular cornmarket in Hawick, and the town's Farmer's Club began the moves which led to the establishment of the fair at Rink which became 'the most extensive fair for draft ewes and wedders in the south of Scotland'.[95] Similarly, in 1828 the members of the Bute Farmers' Society drew up a memorial recommending the establishment of a weekly market in Rothesay. From the funds of the latter society, two weighing machines were purchased and 'placed in such parts of the island as were most in want of these useful auxiliaries to the farmer'.[96] Although co-operative farming had made only slow progress in England by the 1860s,[97] several early Scottish societies had pioneered various schemes fifty years earlier. The use of co-operative methods had resulted in the building of a large granary near the harbour in Macduff by the Buchan and Boyne Farming Society. Erected with funds that had accrued from the astute management of the society's funds, the granary, which was of benefit to both farmers and corn merchants, yielded an annual rent

'equal to the interest of the money laid out on the building and the requisite of the house'.[98] Similarly, one must admire the enterprise of the Forres club which appointed a committee annually to arrange, for the benefit of its members, the importation of coal at a cost considerably less than that charged by the ordinary importers.[99] In conjunction with the members of the Elgin society, the same club formed an establishment at Burghead for the curing and exporting of pork in barrels.[100]

Although most agricultural societies were formed wholly for the dissemination of matters concerned with agriculture, others were concerned with the protection of the agriculturalists themselves. When founded, some societies gave their attention to the problems of the prevention, detection and punishment of crimes committed against their members. Indeed, the minute book of the Penicuik Farmers' Society records that it was not until 1847, some fifty years after its establishment, that 'The usefulness of the Society being now so far superseded by the establishment of the County Police Force it has been deemed expedient to direct the influence of the Society to carry out other objects having a tendency to improve or benefit agriculture'.[101] Again, it is illustrative of the corporate power that could be engendered by such societies (described by George Robertson, the author of the agricultural report of Midlothian, as being 'more unrelenting and inexorable . . . than in an individual')[102] that in the area of the twenty parishes that had joined the Dalkeith Society, which had been founded about 1760 with the express intention of prosecuting thieves, the scale of robberies and petty thefts in 1793 was 'much less frequent than formerly'.[103] Likewise, there were other societies whose objects, although mainly agricultural, also included the provision of finance so that those committing criminal offences against either subscribers or their property could be both apprehended and convicted,[104,105] vagrants brought to justice, and the country's statute acts enforced.[106]

At times, when sheep-worrying by dogs became a nuisance to the local community, the Penicuik society formed a sub-committee to combat the problem. Following interviews with the society's representatives, the individual owners acceded to their requests that the dogs should be destroyed. However, the 'unrelenting and inexorable' actions taken by the clubs were not always directed against outside agencies, and there were occasions when the members had to abide by decisions arising from the internal discipline of their own institution. Provision was made in the rules of the same society for the setting up of an arbitration committee in cases of dispute between members, the decision to be binding on all parties.[107]

Early benefit, or friendly, societies were at times viewed with hostility. The author of a Board of Agriculture report commented that such clubs, 'holden at public houses, increase the number of those houses, and naturally lead to idleness and intemperance; that they afford commodious opportunities to foment sedition, and form illegal combinations'.[108] These latter thoughts, namely that such organisations were politically dangerous, were tempered by the consideration that they could be also instrumental in lowering the poor rate.[109] The development of such organisations was hampered, however, by the lack of reliable sickness and death statistics, which caused the Highland Society in 1820 to appoint a committee to enquire into the state of Friendly Societies.[110] It is probable that societies of the type described above which offered benefits in relation to sickness or death and also mutual insurance in connection with farming activities, as well as advocating agricultural improvement, would have registered later in the century under the Friendly Society Acts.

Founded about 1770, primarily for charitable purposes, the Kilbarchan farmers' society also paid attention to agricultural matters through the distribution of published tracts on topics such as the management of hay and corn harvests etc.[111] Similarly, the society which had been formed in Kincardine about 1793 established a fund for the support of the members' widows and children and, by 1808, could boast a membership of 131 members, a paid clerk and funds in the region of £1,800.[112] The bye-laws drawn up by the Stronsay society in Orkney show similar humanitarian regard for widows and orphans of its members who were left in impoverished circumstances. Here, the subscriptions of the society, which, as noted earlier, were of four different classes, related to the extent of the members' farms, were allowed to accrue for a period of ten years. This residue, after deduction of expenses associated with the quarterly meetings of the society, was intended to help the plight of both widows and orphans, such benefits being in proportion to the original subscriber's payments.[113] The Fife Farming Society, formed about 1794 for the purpose of agricultural improvement, also raised capital for the benefit of widows and children. In addition to helping those who had fallen on hard times because of the death of the family's breadwinner, the Fife society helped those 'reduced to distress or indigence'; however, this allowance of 30 shillings per quarter was not granted when the distress was brought about 'by drunkeness, or any other kind of disorderly conduct'.[114]

The localised studies of the hiring and employing of Scottish agricultural workers by Gray[115] and Devine[116] have illustrated the complex nature of the labour structure in the nineteenth century. Devine[117] has also contrasted the unrest amongst the English rural labouring classes following the end of the Napoleonic Wars with the social stability of the rural lowlands of Scotland. Because the Scottish agricultural employment system included long hires as well as payment in kind, farm servants enjoyed greater security than their English counterparts. Additionally, it has been suggested that this security was more likely to produce greater labour discipline.[118]

By way of confirmation of this latter point, rules regarding the hiring of farm servants were drafted into the regulations of early Scottish agricultural societies. In such cases, membership of a society allowed local agriculturalists to adopt common procedures and policy with regard to the hiring of farm servants. For example, one of the aims of the Banffshire Farming Society when first drawing up its rules in 1785 was to institute a system of fixed fees for such workers.[119] Eight years later, the Lunan and Vinney Water Farming Society's first meeting adopted the proposal that no member should hire a servant without obtaining a recommendation from his former employer.[120] Similarly, the members of both the Nairn and Forres societies undertook to engage the staff of any member of their respective clubs only on production of a certificate indicating 'the wages, discretion, and ability' of the servant.[121] Consideration was not only given to the acquisition of new staff, however, but also to the rewarding of long-service servants. The Deer Society began giving prizes to farm servants in 1796,[122] and the Elgin Farming Club, whose members had adopted a type of uniform in order to encourage the manufacture of cloth at nearby Newmill, extended its gesture to include the gift of a coat of the same cloth to each of the six servants who had served club members continuously over a period of twenty years. Fittingly, the silver buttons on the coats were inscribed 'the reward of faithful service'.[123]

Some societies appear to have successfully inter-married social enjoyment with agricultural enlightenment. Findlater, the author of the agricultural report on Peebles, writes of 'a monthly club, composed chiefly of farmers, that meets at the head inn of the county town for social intercourse'.[124] It was the custom of the Salton Farming Society to commence each meeting with a dinner, five of their regulations being concerned with aspects of the dining arrangements. Far from attracting critical notice, these social preludes were praised by the *Farmer's Magazine*, which considered the society to have displayed 'much judgement . . . considering the dining table . . . as a rallying post around which a full meeting may constantly be expected . . .;[125] such social activities, however, do not appear to have been very common.

Few societies appear to have engendered 'ginger-group' activities, although the Hawick Farmers' Club in 1807 attempted to draw the attention of Government to, as well as to arouse public sympathy for, the 'great hardships sustained by farmers from the hypothetical mode of estimating their profits under the Property Tax Act', their agitation for the repeal or amendment of the tax extending over a period of several years.[126] The same club in 1826 paid from its funds the sum of £8 towards the expense of sending a young man to Edinburgh in order that he should attend the veterinary lectures of William Dick, on condition he settled as a farrier in Hawick on his return.[127] The standards prevailing in both animal medicine and farriery had given concern since the latter part of the eighteenth century. Initially voiced in 1785 by a Hampshire agricultural society, this concern was to give rise to suggestions that veterinary schools should be set up in Britain on a similar basis to those which existed in France, Germany and Scandinavia. Arising from the early endeavours of the Odiham Agricultural Society of Hampshire, the Veterinary College, London was established in 1791 and soon developed a strong membership with a Scottish element that included a future president of the Highland Society (the Duke of Atholl) as well as a number of Scottish peers.[128]

A former student of the London College, William Dick, conscious of the scarcity of veterinary surgeons in Scotland, began in 1819 a series of free lectures in Edinburgh. This course attracted the patronage of the Highland Society which, in addition to giving annual grants in 1833, donated £50 towards the classroom and museum which were part of the new premises then being built at Dick's expense.[129] Six years later the status of the Edinburgh school was changed when it became the Edinburgh College with William Dick as its professor and principal. Later, the early hopes of the Odiham Society were realised, and the generous patronage of the Highland Society rewarded when, in March 1844, under a Charter of Incorporation, the London and Edinburgh colleges were linked under the title of the Royal College of Veterinary Surgeons.[130]

One aspect of the contributions made by local societies which has received little emphasis is that they provided a 'feedback' role by which local grass-root opinions could be collected, collated and disseminated through the medium of farming periodicals, on a national basis. The Highland Society, for example, was 'ready at all times' to pay attention to the opinions of local agricultural societies, 'satisfied that from no source are suggestions likely to be received more deserving of consideration'.[131]

V. *The societies and agricultural literature*

Assuming availability, as well as an interested readership, the publication of agricultural books and periodicals would have stimulated the dissemination of ideas as well as allowing leisured consideration of published empirical observations from which agricultural speculation could be formulated. However, as John Wilson, the author of the agricultural report on Renfrewshire, reflected in 1812, 'the education of many of the farmers in this district, is not so perfect as might be expected, considering the important situation they hold in the community. Few of them are readers of agricultural publications . . .'[132] This situation was further exacerbated by the fact that even when enlightened individuals possessed the motivation to read such literature, the financial means to procure books or periodicals was often lacking. As late as the 1840s the report of the Agricultural Committee of the Fifeshire Literary, Scientific and Antiquarian Society, in support of a resolution that the Society should acquire its own library, noted that

If this library contained the more approved of works on agriculture and science, it would prove exceeding useful, by affording an opportunity to the members of consulting books of reference *which few individuals can afford to purchase for themselves*'[133] (my emphasis). The problems of purchasing the latest farming literature could have been sufficient to turn away all but the wealthy from the paths of improving agriculture. The libraries available to the working class in the early nineteenth century included parochial libraries, subscription libraries, circulating libraries and those attached to Mechanics' Institutes,[134] but it is pertinent to this study to ascertain what steps were taken by agricultural societies to improve the dissemination of agricultural literature.

The acknowledgement made by the Fifeshire Literary, Scientific and Antiquarian Society of the advantages that could arise from the establishment of a library appears to have been recognised also by several agricultural societies. The rules of the Bute Farmers' Society, when drawn up in 1825, indicated that the annual subscription of members should be used 'to constitute a fund, for the purpose of granting Premiums, forming a Library, and otherwise promoting the views of the Society'.[135] Similarly, a society library was a facility enjoyed by the members of the Morayshire Farming Club,[136] the Fettercairn Club,[137] and the Crieff Society.[138] In the early nineteenth century both the Church and the organisers of the parish and institute-type libraries were often very aware of their social 'obligations' regarding the type of literature that should be available to the working man.[139] Whilst the Bible and practical books pertaining to the reader's trades, etc. were acceptable, political works and light fiction were not encouraged. Thus, it is possible that when establisning a library, some agricultural societies could have been persuaded just as much by these paternalistic thoughts as the more obvious ones associated with making available to their members improving agrarian literature.

The more affluent members of the Crieff Society presented the books on farming and rural economy which were the beginnings of the library. The records of several of the societies note similar generous gifts of volumes of agricultural literature that were intended to introduce the rank-and-file membership to the tenets of improving husbandry. Although

expending £2 annually on the employment of a librarian, the Strathearn Agricultural Society experienced problems arising from the loss of books. Because the librarian was financially responsible for such losses, the society found it necessary to raise his annual salary to £10![140]

The graph of publication of agricultural books and periodicals that were published in Scotland, or known to have been read in Scotland, rose considerably from the latter quarter of the eighteenth century.[141] However, publication is not necessarily synonymous with the worthiness of the contents. In 1781 Arthur Young wrote that in 'hundreds of our books of husbandry . . . the writers assert facts that we now know to be nearly impossible'.[142] In view of this comment, it is relevant to enquire which of the printed works of the period found their way into the libraries that were established by some agricultural societies. As may be imagined, there is a comparative scarcity of information about the printed works held in their libraries. Nevertheless, assuming that the income of the societies arose mainly from subscriptions and therefore that care would be exercised in the selection of books for purchase, it is of interest to consider the reading matter that was considered relevant and which was available to the membership. Where records still exist, mention can be found of the Board of Agriculture reports and the various volumes of the *Farmer's Magazine*,[143] the *Northern Agricultural Magazine*,[144] the Highland Society's *Prize Essays and Transactions, The Farmers' Register*,[145] Lord Kames' *The Gentleman Farmer, Letters and Papers . . . of the Bath and West of England Society*, and Dickson's *A Treatise of Agriculture*.[146] Only a very few societies appear to have produced their own publications, prompted in the main by the enthusiasm and endeavours of an individual rather than the corporate work of the group. About 1772 the Rev. John Warner, minister of Kilbarchan, published and circulated agricultural tracts which had been prepared for the benefit of members of the farmers' society of that parish.[147] Later, under the enthusiastic editorship of Samuel Girdwood, the Bute Farmers' Society produced a periodical publication, the *Bute Record of Rural Affairs*, which first appeared in November 1839.[148] Thus, by these various means, a few of the agricultural societies would have aided interested individuals who, ordinarily, would have been thwarted by lack of access, arising from shortage of finance, to new farming publications. In making available selected books and periodicals as well as the very important means by which contemporary topics could be debated with fellow farmers, the societies provided forms of self-education within the framework of what basically were agricultural seminars.

VI.   *The life span of the societies*

As has been shown, societies which were fostering agricultural ideas could be found in many areas of Scotland, and some counties could boast a liberal scattering of such clubs. It is almost impossible to guess the number of agricultural societies that existed in Scotland prior to 1835, the terminal date of this study. Published references to such societies do not often include details of their foundation dates, and their demise is very seldom recorded. Additionally, little documentary evidence appears to have survived. Both Fox and Goddard have commented on the rapid expansion of English and Welsh societies during the nineteenth century.[149] However, although a similar rise took place in Scotland, the period of proliferation appears to have occurred earlier. Of the Scottish societies with known establishment dates that have been examined here, over half were formed during the period 1790-1810. Many of the societies enjoyed only short active lives. By 1824, for example, the societies that had preceded the Highland Society had all been disbanded, and it was able to claim that it was the oldest of Scottish agricultural associations.[150] Therefore, one must ask what factors contributed to the demise of many of these societies.

Undoubtedly during this period of agricultural improvement too many small societies were established — in 1808 the county and parochial societies were 'so numerous as to set calculation at defiance'[151] — and it is likely that the enthusiasm and endeavours of many agricultural communities were weakened by the processes of fragmentation. One wonders about the strained loyalties of those farming in the Annandale region who supported an Agricultural Society, an upper-district Agricultural Society, a Farmers' Society and a Society for Promoting Improvements. However, while recognising that too many societies were formed to enjoy the sustained support of the agricultural community, we must also acknowledge J. W. Hudson's observation that 'Institutions, like all great works, flourish or decay in

proportion to their value and utility to the age in which they exist'.[152] The *Farmer's Magazine* in 1850 considered that the demise of many small associations was a trend that was not to be altogether regretted.[153] In the beginning, when so much agricultural improvement had been required, such organisations had been most useful, for they had introduced new standards to both cultivators and breeders, inducing them to lift themselves from 'the slough of inactive supineness in which too many were willing to rest'. Since those early times, farmers had developed both their ideas and standards, and greater attention was being paid to the centralisation of societies within localities, the provincial and county societies flourishing at the expense of the small associations. Thus, although some clubs were forced to fold, others such as the Tweedside Agricultural Society and the Border Society were strengthened by amalgamation.[154] Not surprisingly, a lot were dissolved in the wake of the periods of agricultural depression.[155] The Caithness society was forced to disband when the calls of service to 'King and Country, in Fencible Corps, etc'.[156] depleted its membership, whilst the prestigious and thriving society at Dumfries was dissolved in the wake of the failure of the Ayr Bank,[157] an event which 'threw a general damp upon the spirits of the people'.[158]

Just as the influence of the societies tended to be local, the reasons for the disbandment of many societies were also local. For example, internal migration of native-born Scots had reached a high level by 1851, a factor that would have caused fluctuations in the membership of societies, especially those that were both small and situated in rural areas.[159] Also, much would have depended on the quality and enthusiasm of the officers of the local society, especially where the society was founded through the individual talents and enthusiasm of one particular individual. The Lunan and Vinney Water Farming Society serves as a good example, and illustrates both the strength and weakness of societies relying on one individual. Founded in 1803 under the auspices of George Dempster of Dunnichen, its meetings appear to have been dominated by his enthusiasm and agricultural knowledge, which led to his early appointment as 'Perpetual Preses'.[160] Although apparently still flourishing, no further meeting was held after the occasion of the society's twelfth anniversary in 1814. At this time Dempster was in his eightieth year and possibly unable to carry out his duties as president and, in the words of a later writer, 'it may have been deemed ungracious to choose a substitute'.[161] Ironically, the eventual demise of certain societies in the counties of Roxburgh and Selkirk stemmed in part from their decision to hold their meetings on market days. Although such an arrangement was convenient for the farming membership which foregathered on these occasions, the business of the societies was punctuated by the comings and goings of the membership, 'who naturally preferred the settlement of a heavy account, the making of an advantageous bargain, and above all the receipt of money, to the most interesting debate or conversation'.[162] Such interruptions so extended the business of the society's meetings that the members, then requiring sustenance, dined together so late into the evening that it was commented that 'they did more service to the inn than to agriculture'.[163]

Instances of dissension within societies are seldom recorded in their minutes, and it is difficult to ascertain if the case of the Banffshire Farming Society was unusual. Here, 'politics usurped the place of the plough', causing thinly attended meetings, and with funds diluted by tavern bills, the society was forced to disband.[164]

VII. *Agricultural societies: their role and achievements*
The establishment of farming societies took place at a time when Scottish reformers were giving emphasis to the structural changes that could lead to a 'new' agriculture, one that was both technologically improved as well as more capital intensive.[165] Under the pressure of a growing population, agrarian development was being shaped by the need for greater market production. By the beginning of the eighteenth century, this agricultural commercialisation had brought about unprecedented growth in the number of market centres.[166] To what extent did the growth of early agricultural societies speed the advance of agrarian improvement in Scotland?

Just as it is not easy to arrive at a precise evaluation of the endeavours of the early agricultural pioneers, it is also difficult to pinpoint the precise achievements of the agricultural societies. At times, the success of both of these influences was denigrated by contemporary writers. When discussing the agricultural efforts of 'several men of genius', the preface of *Present State of Husbandry in Scotland,* published in 1778,

commented that 'their success has hitherto produced few imitators',[167] whilst George Robertson, in his *Rural Recollections,* notes that there was little evidence that Cockburn of Ormiston's East Lothian Society had 'any considerable influence in the improvement of the country'.[168] References to early agricultural societies are to be found amongst the writings of the Improvers and, therefore, are open to the modern charge of being possibly inaccurate and biased. In this study, an attempt has been made to restrict the references that illustrate the roles of agricultural societies to fact rather than eulogistic comment.

Although perhaps it is easier merely to accept mention of such men and societies as indicating that the topic of agricultural improvement was exciting attention rather than bringing about specific local or national changes, even in the light of scanty data it is clear that such societies provided a service to Scottish agriculture by diffusing, in piecemeal fashion, improving knowledge. Similarly, it may be asserted that the societies, through collective action, achieved more than would have been possible through the individual endeavours of their membership. Providing that recognition is given to the factor of local variation, certain generalisations can also be made with regard to both their role and achievements:

1. The early development of the Scottish agricultural society movement was in advance of that of England.
2. The agricultural societies harnessed the developing feeling of national pride and, additionally, became the vehicles by which men of the landed classes could, by their leadership, attempt to emulate the higher standards of English farming.
3. By acting as forums of agricultural discussion between those of different classes, the societies became agents of change, providing opportunities for innovation in areas of agricultural conservatism whilst, at the same time, stimulating the farming community by introducing the element of competition. In many cases, the societies provided the educational or instructional means by which those towards the base of the agricultural pyramid, who sometimes could neither read nor had the means to travel, could learn about new techniques, crops, implements, etc.
4. Certain societies pioneered, with success, aspects of co-operative farming. Other institutions diversi-

fied their activities in order to combat rural crime and acted as agricultural friendly societies to relieve cases of local distress.

5. Through the medium of society pamphlets, local newspapers and agricultural journals, many societies provided the means by which the voice of *local* farming communities could be heard.

References

1. S. Macdonald, 'The diffusion of knowledge among Northumberland farmers, 1780-1815', *The Agricultural History Review*, 27, 1979, pp. 30-39.

2. K. Hudson, *Patriotism with profit*, London, 1972.

3. H. S. A. Fox, 'Local farmers' associations and the circulation of agricultural information in nineteenth-century England', in H. S. A. Fox and R. A. Butlin (eds.), *Change in the countryside: essays on rural England, 1500-1900*, London, 1979.

4. N. P. W. Goddard, 'Agricultural Societies', in G. E. Mingay (ed.), *The Victorian Countryside*, London, 1981, vol. 1, pp. 245-259.

5. N. P. W. Goddard, The Royal Agricultural Society of England and agricultural progress 1838-1880, unpub. Ph.D. thesis, University of Kent at Canterbury, 1981.

6. J. E. Handley, *The Agricultural Revolution in Scotland*, Glasgow, 1963.

7. J. A. Symon, *Scottish Farming Past and Present*, Edinburgh, 1959.

8. T. Bedford Franklin, *A History of Scottish Farming*, Edinburgh, 1952.

9. A. Ramsay, *History of the Highland and Agricultural Society of Scotland*, Edinburgh, 1879.

10. A. M'Callum, 'The Society of Improvers', *The Scottish Journal of Agriculture*, XVIII, 1935, pp. 40-47.

11. J. H. Smith, *The Gordon's Mill Farming Club 1758-1764*, Aberdeen, 1962.

12. R. L. Emerson, 'The Social composition of enlightened Scotland: the select society of Edinburgh, 1754-1764', *Studies of Voltaire and the Eighteenth Century*, CXIV, 1973, pp. 291-329.

13. A. Y., 'Agricultural Societies', *Annals of Agriculture*, 40, 1803, pp. 476-7.

14. Societies were noted in Banff, Glasgow, Edinburgh, Perth and Ross-shire.

15. *Letters and Papers . . . of the Bath and West of England Society*, 12, 1810, pp. 396-403.

16. *Letters and Papers . . . of the Bath and West of England Society*, 12, 1810, p. xviii.

17. *Ibid.*, p. vi.

18. R. Maxwell, *Select Transactions of the Honourable The Society of Improvers in the Knowledge of Agriculture in Scotland*, Edinburgh, 1743, p. xvi.

19. *Ibid.*, p. xviii.

20. *Ibid.*.

21. *A Treatise concerning the manner of Fallowing of Ground, Raising of Grass-seeds, and Training of Lint and Hemp*, Edinburgh, 1724.

22. R. Maxwell, 'The Practical Husbandman: being a collection of miscellaneous papers on husbandry', Edinburgh, 1757.

23. Maxwell, 1743, *op. cit.*, p. x.

24. J. A. S. Watson and G. D. Amery, 'Early Scottish agricultural writers (1697-1790)', *Transactions of the Highland and Agricultural Society of Scotland* (hereafter *T.H.A.S.*), XLIII, 1931, p. 67.

25. *A True Method of treating Light Hazely Ground; or, an exact relation of the Practice of Farmers in Buchan, containing Rules for Infields, Outfields, Haughs, and Laighs, By a small Society of Farmers in Buchan*, Edinburgh, 1735.

26. D. Souter, *General View of the Agriculture of the County of Banff*, Edinburgh, 1812, Appendix vi.

27. *Ibid.*, p. 34.

28. Ramsay, *op. cit.*, p. 58.

29. J. B. Caird, 'The making of the Scottish rural landscape', *Scottish Geographical Magazine*, 80, 1964, pp. 72-80.

30. G. Whittington, 'Was there a Scottish Agricultural Revolution?', *Area*, 7, 1975, pp. 204-206.

31. D. Mills, 'A Scottish agricultural revolution?', *Area*, 8, 1976, p. 237.

32. M. L. Parry, *Ibid.*, pp. 238-9.

33. I. H. Adams, 'The agricultural revolution in Scotland: contributions to the debate', *Area*, 10, 1978, pp. 198-203.

34. I. D. Whyte, *Ibid.*, pp. 203-5.

35. Fox, *op. cit.*, p. 58, note 26.

36. H. S. A. Fox, *op. cit.*, p. 58 (note 25), suggests that only one local farmers' association was instituted in England before the mid-eighteenth century, and cites P. G. Selby, *The Faversham Farmers' Club and its members*, 1927.

37. M. L. Parry and T. R. Slater, *The Making of the Scottish Countryside*, London, 1980.

38. I. H. Adams, 'The agents of agricultural change', in *Ibid.*, p. 170.

39. T. C. Smout and A. Fenton, 'Scottish agriculture before the Improvers, an exploration', *Agricultural History Review*, 13, 1965, 73-93.

40. Whittington, *op. cit.*

41. Whyte, *op. cit.*

42. Whyte, 1980, 'The emergence of the new estate structure', in Parry and Slater, *op. cit.*

43. Souter, *op. cit.*, p. 34.

44. Souter, *op. cit.*, p. 326.

45. J. Robertson, *General View of the Agriculture in the Southern Districts of the County of Perth*, London, 1794, p. 131.

46. J. Sinclair, *Analysis of the Statistical Account of Scotland*, 1831, p. 303.

47. *The New Statistical Account of Scotland* (hereafter *N.S.A.*), 13, 1845, p. 336.

48. Ramsay, *op. cit.*, p. 118.

49. *T.H.A.S.*, 5, 1820, p. lvii.

50. *N.S.A.*, *op. cit.*, p. 336.

51. Fox, *op. cit.*, p. 46.

52. *Ibid.*, p. 46.

53. Goddard, *op. cit.*, p. 252.

54. Smith, *op. cit.*, p. 9.

55. *Farmer's Magazine*, Dec. 1808, p. 464.

56. Rev. J. Thomson, *General View of the Agriculture of Fife*, Edinburgh, 1800.

57. Ramsay, *op. cit.*, p. 160.

58. Souter, *op. cit.*, p. 327.

59. Souter, *op. cit.*, p. 325.

60. *Aberdeen Magazine*, 1761, p. 13.

61. *Transactions of the Society for the Encouragement of Agriculture within the Counties of Dumfries and Wigton, and Stewartry of Kirkcudbright*, Dumfries, 1776, p iii.

62. Smith, *op. cit.*, p. vi.

63. Correspondence from Arthur Young published in A. Wight, *Present State of Husbandry in Scotland*, 4, pt 2, Edinburgh, 1784, p. 698.

64. *Aberdeen Magazine*, I, 1761, p. 153.

65. P. Graham, *General View of the Agriculture of Stirlingshire*, Edinburgh, 1812, p. 383.

66. J. Fergusson (ed.), *Letters of George Dempster to Sir Adam Fergusson 1756-1813*, London, 1934.

67. Rev. C. Rogers, 'Jottings from the records of a farming society in the County of Forfar, 1803-1814, ... *Proceedings of the Society of Antiquaries of Scotland*, 16, 1881-2, p. 234.

68. Fergusson, *op. cit.*, p. 252.

69. *Ibid.*, p. 290.

70. *The Elgin Courant and Courier*, Nov. 11, 1898, p. 6.

71. J. Robson, *General View of the Agriculture in the County of Argyll and Western Part of Inverness-shire*, London, 1794, Appendix 1, p. 53.

72. *The Statistical Account of Scotland*, The Orkney Parishes, p. 308.

73. *N.S.A.* (Kincardineshire), p. 123.

74. Ramsay, *op. cit.*, p. 209.

75. W. B. Martin, *The Farmers of Bute for 60 years and beyond*, 1951, p. 11.

76. *Farmer's Magazine*, Dec. 1808, p. 464.

77. Sinclair, 1831, *op. cit.*, p. 303.

78. *Greenock Advertiser*, 11th March, 1803, p. 4, col. 1.

79. Graham, *op. cit.*, p. 383.

80. Rev. A. Whyte and D. MacFarlan, *General View of the Agriculture of the County of Dumbarton*, Glasgow, 1811 p. 309.

81. Graham, *op. cit.*, p. 384.

82. W. M. Metcalfe, *A History of the County of Renfrew from the Earliest of Times*, Paisley, 1905, p. 355.

83. J. W. Hudson, *The History of Adult Education*, 1851 (1969 ed.), p. 165.

84. A Minute of the Garioch Club, 1811. Aberdeen University Library, MS 3064, Bundle 196. I am indebted to Dr. D. B. Johnston, Aberdeen University Library, for this reference.

85. *Clydesdale Journal*, May 18, 1821.

86. *Aberdeen Magazine*, I, 1761, p. 14.

87. D. D. Black, *The History of Brechin*, Brechin, 1839, pp. 196 and 279.

88. I am indebted to Mrs E. Marrison for this reference to the activities of the Kintyre Farmers Society.

89. *Farmer's Magazine*, 1808, p. 372.

90. *Articles and Regulations of the Corresponding and Improving Society of Farmers in Renfrewshire*, Paisley, 1788, p. 3.

91. *Aberdeen Magazine*, I, 1761, p. 154.

92. *Ibid.*, p. 154.

93. Souter, *op. cit.*, p. 328.

94. A. B. Barty, *The History of Dunblane*, Stirling, 1944, p. 245.

95. *N.S.A.*, 3, *op. cit.*, p. 402.

96. *N.S.A.*, (Rothesay) *op. cit.*, p. 109.

97. Goddard, *op. cit.*, p. 255.

98. Souter, *op. cit.*, p. 331.

99. Rev. W. Leslie, *General View of the Agriculture of the Counties of Nairn and Moray*, London, 1811, p. 443.

100. *Ibid.*

101. I am indebted to Mr W. J. Ross for drawing my attention to this reference.

102. G. Robertson, *General View of the Agriculture of the County of Midlothian*, Edinburgh, 1793, p. 76.

103. *Ibid.*

104. Rev. R. Douglas, *General View of the Agriculture of the Counties of Roxburgh and Selkirk*, Edinburgh, 1798, p. 353.

105. *Articles and Regulations of the . . . Society of Farmers in Renfrewshire*, 1788, p. 7.

106. Souter, *op. cit.*, p. 328.

107. See note 101.

108. Quoted in P. H. J. H. Gosden, *The Friendly Societies in England*, Manchester, 1961, p. 3.

109. *Ibid.*, p. 6.

110. 'Report of the Committee of the Highland Society of Scotland, appointed in 1820 to inquire into the state of Friendly Societies; ... *T.H.A.S.*, 6, 1824, pp. 271-560.

111. J. Wilson, *General View of the Agriculture of Renfrewshire*, Paisley, 1812, p. 351.

112. G. Robertson, *General View of the Agriculture of Kincardineshire*, London, 1808, p. 451.

113. *S.A.S.*, Orkney Parishes, *op. cit.*, p. 308.

114. J. Thomson, *General View of the Agriculture of the County of Fife*, 1800.

115. M. Gray, 'North-East agriculture and the labour force, 1790-1875', in A. A. Maclaren (ed.), *Social Class in Scotland: Past and Present*, Edinburgh, 1976.

116. T. M. Devine, 'The demand for agricultural labour in East Lothian after the Napoleonic Wars', *Transactions of the East Lothian Antiquarian and Field Naturalists Society*, 16, 1979, pp. 49-61.

117. T. M. Devine, 'Social stability and agrarian change in the eastern lowlands of Scotland, 1810-1840', *Social History*, 3, 1978, pp. 331-346.

118. *Ibid.*, p. 336.

119. Souter, *op. cit.*, p. 327.

120. Rogers, *op. cit.*, p. 232.

121. Leslie, *op. cit.*, p. 442.

122. Ramsay, *op. cit.*, p. 87.

123. Leslie, *op. cit.*, p. 444.

124. Rev. C. Findlater, *General View of the Agriculture of the County of Peebles*, Edinburgh, 1802, p. 256.

125. *Farmer's Magazine*, Sept. 1808, p. 374.

126. *N.S.A.*, 3, *op. cit.*, p. 402.

127. *N.S.A.*, 3, *op. cit.*, p. 403.

128. L. P. Pugh, *Farriery to Veterinary Medicine*, 1962, p. 43.

129. Pugh, *op. cit.*, p. 120.

130. Pugh, *op. cit.*, p. 126.

131. *T.H.A.S.*, 6, 1824, p. lii.

132. Wilson, *op. cit.*, p. 349.

133. J. Brodie, 'Report of the Agricultural Committee', *Fifeshire Literary, Scientific and Antiquarian Society*, 1840.

134. A. R. Thompson, 'The use of Libraries by the Working Class in Scotland in the Early Nineteenth Century', *Scottish Historical Review*, 42, 1963, 21-29.

135. S. Girdwood, *Bute Record of Rural Affairs*, Rothesay, 1860, p. 91.

136. 'Centenary of Morayshire Farming Club', *The Elgin Courant and Courier*, November 15th, 1898, p. 6.

137. *N.S.A.*, Kincardine, *op. cit.*, p. 123.

138. Rev. J. Robertson, *General View of the Agriculture of the County of Perth*, Perth, 1813, p. 430.

139. J. W. Hudson, *History of Adult Education*, 1851, p. 196.

140. A. Porteous, *The History of Crieff*, Edinburgh, 1812, p. 166.

141. Adams, 1980, *op. cit.*, p. 172.

142. Correspondence from Arthur Young published in A. Wight, *op. cit.*, p. 698.

143. Leslie, *op. cit.*, p. 444.

144. *Elgin Courant and Courier*, Nov. 15, 1898, p. 6.

145. Girdwood, *op. cit.*, p. 93.

146. See note 88.

147. Wilson, *op. cit.*, p. 351.

148. Martin, *op. cit.*, p. 13.

149. Fox, *op. cit.*, p. 46, has estimated that the number of English agricultural societies rose seventeen-fold in the period 1800-75. Goddard, *op. cit.*, p. 246, has suggested a seven-fold increase between 1835 and 1855.

150. *T.H.A.S.*, 6, 1824, p. lii.

151. *The Farmer's Magazine*, 9, 1808, p. 97.

152. J. W. Hudson, *op. cit.*, p. 168.

153. *The Farmer's Magazine*, 16, 1850, p. 537.

154. The Tweedside Agricultural Society, formed in 1803, and the Border Society, established in 1812, amalgamated in 1820 under the new title of the Union Agricultural Society. *The Southern Counties' Register and Directory*, Kelso, 1866, p. 89.

155. *T.H.A.S.*, 6, 1824, p. lii.

156. J. Henderson, *General View of the Agriculture of the County of Caithness*, London, 1812, p. 267.

157. Douglas Heron and Company collapsed in June 1772 (see H. Hamilton, 'The Failure of the Ayr Bank, 1772', *Economic History Review*, 8, 1955-6, pp. 405-417).

158. J. Webster, *General View of the Agriculture of Galloway*, Edinburgh, 1794, p. 14.

159. M. Gray, 'Scottish Emigration: The Social Impact of Agrarian Change in the Rural Lowlands, 1775-1875', *Perspectives in American History*, 7, 1973, pp. 95-174.

160. Rogers, *op. cit.*, p. 231.

161. *Ibid.*, p. 235.

162. Douglas, *op. cit.*, p. 352.

163. *Ibid.*, p. 353.

164. *N.S.A.*, 13, *op. cit.*, p. 336.

165. E. J. Hobsbawm, 'Scottish reformers of the eighteenth century and capitalist agriculture', in *Peasants in History: Essays in Honour of Daniel Thorner*, Calcutta, 1980, pp. 3-29.

166. I. Whyte, 'Progress to a modern world', *Geographical Magazine*, July 1979, p. 699.

167. Wight, *op. cit.*, vol. 1, 1778 edition, p. vii.

168. G. Robertson, *Rural Recollections*, Irvine, 1829, p. 13.

Notes

The Romans in Scotland

D J Breeze

The Romans are in fashion! The production of several school packs on the Romans in Scotland, the revamping of the displays of Roman material at two of Scotland's major museums, the success of television serials (for both children and adults) about the Romans and the opening of new ancient monuments of the Roman period are all testimony to this. The reasons for this upsurge in interest are not my concern, though the Romans have always had a certain fascination: my intention is rather to examine the fruits of this aroused interest.

Both the National Museum of Antiquities of Scotland (NMAS) and the Hunterian Museum in the University of Glasgow have recently reorganised their exhibitions of Roman material. The Roman Room in the National Museum has been modernised − this included the insertion of a false ceiling − with the exhibits rearranged in topics such as the army, cooking, building, etc. To coincide with the reopening of the Roman Room the National Museum produced a guide to the Roman collections. Entitled *The Romans in Scotland*, this is available from the National Museum, Queen Street, Edinburgh, price £3.

The exhibition of Roman material at the Hunterian Museum has to fit into rather more cramped surroundings in the main gallery of the museum. Nevertheless, the principal jewels of the collection − the distance slabs from the Antonine Wall − are displayed to good effect, while the cases include many recent discoveries donated to the museum. The museum's bookstall offers a range of books and booklets pertaining to the Romans in Scotland as well as slides and postcards (from September 1983 a further addition to the bookstall was a wall chart on Bearsden Roman fort, prepared by David Thornborrow, and costing £1: available from Dr. L. J. F. Keppie, Hunterian Museum, The University, Glasgow G12 8QQ).

The Roman collections of the Hunterian Museum were reorganised for the visit to the museum of the Congress of Roman Frontier Studies in 1979. Also produced for this visit was a guide to Roman sites in Scotland. This booklet, 64 pages long, contains a gazetteer of all visible Roman sites in Scotland as well as suggested tours and a list of museums displaying Roman objects in Scotland (D. J. Breeze, *Roman Scotland: A Guide to the Visible Remains*, published by Frank Graham, 6 Queen's Terrace, Newcastle-upon-Tyne, price £1.20).

A somewhat different level of information is provided by the school packs. So far three have come to my attention. Two are specifically related to museum collections (NMAS and Hunterian), while the third is more wide-ranging and also contains a tape-slide set. The Hunterian Museum's pack, *The Romans in Scotland AD 80-200*, subtitled *Information for Teachers*, is the only in-house product. *The Romans in Scotland, Museum Unit* is related to the Roman Room at the National Museum of Antiquities, but is prepared by the Lothian Regional Council, Department of Education, Advisory Service Division. The third pack, which is altogether more ambitious, is prepared by the Classical Studies Unit of Renfrew and Dunbarton Divisions' Education Resource Service.

All three packs contain the same basic information: guidelines for visits, guide to the museum, synopses of projects, book lists, information concerning loan kits (Renfrew and Dunbarton's pack includes their tape-slide set), work sheet for pupils. However, the balance within each pack is different. Not surprisingly, the Hunterian's emphasis is on the visit to the museum (a delightful bonus here is the availability at the museum of 11 reproduction Roman costumes for the children to try on), but it also offers suggestions on a follow-up to the visit. Lothian Regional Council's pack is perhaps more concerned with this latter aspect, containing many suggestions for further

1. The bath-house at Bearsden looking south from the balcony of one of the adjacent flats. Along the spine of the bath-house, from right to left, lie the changing room, cold room, two warm rooms, steam room and furnace. The hot dry room (with its own furnace) lies to this side of the cold room, and the apsidal cold bath the other. The latrine is to the top left, while part of an earlier bath-house is visible bottom right.

activities, details of the loan kits available, and the best bibliography. Renfrew and Dunbarton's pack provides work programmes for a visit to Bar Hill fort and the Hunterian Museum (more are in preparation), and information about other museums and sites to visit. In addition, there is an 87-page booklet, aimed at pupils rather than teachers, covering all aspects of the building and history of the Wall, the life of soldiers stationed on it, a section on their British opponents and three stories, all interleaved with exercises and 'extra assignments'. Finally, an added dimension is provided by the set of 50 slides provided with written commentary which is repeated on tape.

Many of these slides are of monuments, some in England; some north of the Border. The range of Romano-Scottish sites to visit has increased dramatically over the last two years, in particular in the Glasgow area.

1982 saw the centenary of the passing of the first Ancient Monuments Act. As part of the celebrations to mark this anniversary Mr Allan Stewart, MP, Minister for Home Affairs and the Environment at the Scottish Office, opened the newly consolidated bath-house at Bearsden to the public. In his address Mr Stewart noted that this ancient monument, now in the ownership of the Secretary of State for Scotland, was the first Roman stone building to be placed on display in Scotland. The bath-house lies on Roman Road in the centre of Bearsden, and is open at all times (Fig. 1). To compensate for the lack of a custodian, a rather more detailed level of visitor interpretation is provided at the monument, with an interpretative panel, which contains reconstruction drawings of the fort and the bath-house, being

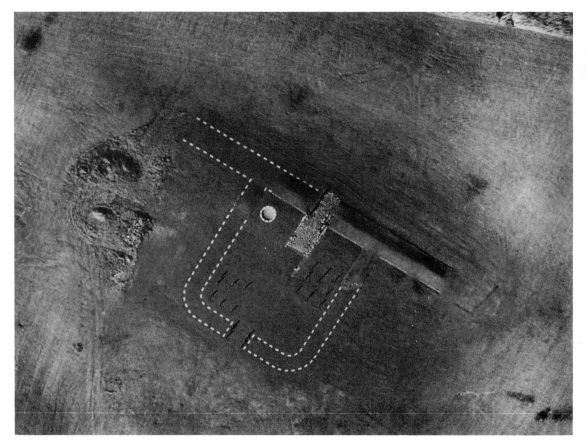

2. The fortlet at Kinneil from the air. The parts of the rampart now destroyed are picked out in paving slabs. Modern timbers have been placed in the sockets of their Roman predecessors. The well lies in the top left-hand corner of the fortlet.

supplemented by small on-site notices. A guide leaflet to the bath-house is also available from either the Hunterian Museum or the Lillie Art Gallery in Milngavie, though there are plans to place a dispenser on site at Bearsden.

Roman bath-houses are in vogue at present. The Scottish Development Department has recently consolidated the small bath-house within the fort at Bar Hill on the Antonine Wall as well as the head-quarters building within the fort. Work on landscaping here is not yet completed, while the plans for the interpretation of the site to the public have yet to be finalised.

A further project nearing completion is the rebuilding of the Roman bath-house at Bothwellhaugh in Strathclyde Country Park. Here the bath-house was flooded by the construction of a new lake, and the local authority, Motherwell District Council, working with the Manpower Services

Commission, have re-excavated the bath-house and rebuilt it at a high level, above the water level. This work, completed during the course of 1983, should provide a notable attraction for visitors to the Park.

The final site requiring mention lies to the east, at Bo'ness at the eastern end of the Antonine Wall. Here Falkirk Museum, also working in collaboration with the Manpower Services Commission, have excavated and consolidated a fortlet on the Wall at Kinneil (Fig. 2). This is the first Roman fortlet to be laid open for public inspection on the line of the Wall, and indeed the only fortlet visible. An exhibition describing the excavation and displaying the finds from it is in the small museum at Kinneil.

School packs, slides, postcards, guide books and new ancient monuments are all witness to the vitality of Roman studies in Scotland. It is especially encouraging that the renewed interest crosses all age barriers. Long may it flourish!

A Scottish Historical Atlas

R G Cant

When work was proceeding on the *Historical Atlas of Scotland* – eventually published in 1975* – considerable thought was given to its form and content. Since it was produced as one of the research projects of the Conference of Scottish Mediaevalists, it was natural that its chronological span should be limited to the period from c.400 to c.1600 A.D. and that its main emphasis should be on political, ecclesiastical, and economic history. Furthermore, as the funds available for its production were extremely limited and its sales prospects somewhat doubtful, it was agreed that the maps should be in simple uncoloured outline and the accompanying texts made as economically succinct as possible.

In the outcome the sales of the completed work have far exceeded the most sanguine expectations of its promoters and, after two reprints, consideration is now being given to the preparation of an entirely new edition, probably of more extended chronological coverage and dealing rather more comprehensively with the various aspects of Scottish history.

It is in itself an interesting historical fact that the notion of reconstructing the character of earlier civilisations in map form was present almost from the beginnings of modern cartography in the sixteenth century. In the British Isles William Camden included historical as well as topographical maps in his *Britannia* (1586 : 1607), likewise his disciple John Speed in his more comprehensive *Theatre of the Empire of Great Britain,* produced as part of his *History of Great Britain* published in 1611-12.

Characteristically, if understandably, these works paid little attention to Scotland, where the systematic surveying and mapping of the country began on the individual initiative of Timothy Pont around 1600. While his concern was primarily topographical, Pont recorded some of the more remarkable 'ancient monuments', as did his successors Robert and James Gordon under the direction of their cantankerous but public-spirited and fortunately long-lived patron, Sir John Scot of Scotstarvit. He it was who saw to the publication of their work in a separate Scottish volume of Johan Blaeu's *Atlas Novus* – with general maps of contemporary and 'ancient' Scotland – in 1654. In 1684, too, Sir Robert Sibbald, with the help of the cartographer John Adair, brought out a survey of the natural history of the country in his *Scotia Illustrata.*

Against this background it is perhaps not surprising, a century later, to find the 11th Earl of Buchan (in 1780) founding a Society of Antiquaries of Scotland having as one of its prime objectives the compilation of a comprehensive survey of all features contributing to its distinctive identity, General William Roy (in 1784) inaugurating what would become the Ordnance Survey, and Sir John Sinclair (between 1791 and 1799) inspiring and editing the first truly modern *Statistical Account* of any country. At a later date the Edinburgh map-making firms of Johnston and Bartholomew were in the very forefront of cartographic publishing, the former being involved in the production of Bevan's *Statistical Atlas of England, Scotland, and Ireland* in 1882 and the latter in the Royal Scottish Geographical Society's superb *Atlas of Scotland* in 1895.

Ideally, a historical atlas should supply a series of cross-sections, at regular intervals, of every significant aspect of the life of the particular society with which it is concerned. That is to say, it should do several times over what the 'national atlases' of recent years have done to portray the complete ethnological identity of the land in question. For countries of comparable scale to Scotland, those of Finland (1960), Austria (1961 onwards), the Netherlands

* *An Historical Atlas of Scotland c.400-c.1600.* Edited by Peter McNeill and Ranald Nicholson. Atlas Committee of the Conference of Scottish Mediaevalists per Department of Mediaeval History, The University, St. Andrews, KY16 9AJ. 1975. £3.00.

(1965-77), and Switzerland (1965-78) provide representative examples.

An inherent difficulty here is that the statistics on which these works are based become more and more meagre the further back we go. Indeed, with the notable exception of Sweden they are rarely available in any very satisfactory form much before 1800. To take such a fundamental matter as population and its distribution, the first official census of Great Britain was made only in 1801. Before this, in Scotland, Sir John Sinclair and his correspondents worked hard to provide accurate figures for the 1790s, as did Alexander Webster in the 1750s, but further back we have little more than estimates based on scanty and fallible information. Even so, one must be grateful for such efforts as that of Lord Cooper (in 1947) to calculate the population of Scotland in the thirteenth century.

In this field, then, so fundamental to the understanding of the quality of life in a particular country at a particular period, all we can do is to record settlements in the light of their geographical location and with the assistance of such archaeological and documentary evidence as may be available. From a study of place-names, too, it may be possible to determine their ethnic character and to assess the probable political composition of an entire area.

This was the approach of the *Historical Atlas of Scotland* to the initial part of its survey − prior to political unification in its definitive form, the beginnings of 'administrative documentation', and the development of more sophisticated building techniques in the eleventh century. From this point onwards it becomes possible to map and interpret the main constituent elements in Scottish life with reasonable accuracy − royal, feudal, burghal, and ecclesiastical organisation, with the changes that came in successive historical periods.

In an atlas of this particular size and character it would be difficult to ask for much more than is provided. And if there are occasional oddities of omission and inclusion, these are of slight account alongside the lucid exposition, often for the first time and sometimes in considerable detail, of matters essential to a comprehension of Scottish history for students, teachers, and researchers at all levels. Furthermore, the simple black and white cartography, austere as it may seem, at least avoids the misleading impressions conveyed by certain maps depicting a whole area in one bright colour regardless of its demographic content, the quality of its social and governmental organisation, or the other factors that determine its identity.

In the new edition now contemplated the texts and maps will be placed next to each other, the chronological span will be extended to 1707, and the topical coverage enlarged. It would also be of immense value if the promoters could enlist the co-operation of their modern colleagues to provide a comparable survey of the ensuing period. For this, a great deal of the specialist groundwork has already been completed in recent years in a whole variety of fields, so that the task should not be unduly daunting.

It may, of course, be argued that a fully representative survey might be unduly ambitious, and recondite, in a historical atlas of necessarily moderate dimensions and price. If so, has the time not come to consider the production of a National Atlas of Scotland comparable to that of Sweden (1953-71)? And if we cannot match that country's unique range of statistical source-material, there is no question that such an enterprise could command the kinds of specialist expertise necessary for the task and surely fully the equal of that now involved (since 1980) in the production of *The National Atlas of Wales*.

Reviews

Land and Society in Early Scotland, Oxford 1982,
345 pp. £27.50
R A Dodgshon

Dodgshon's book is an attempt at the synthesis of studies of
the relationship between social structures and patterns of
occupation in 'Early Scotland'; from the prehistoric period
to the 'eve of the Improvers' Movement' in the mid-
eighteenth century: 'only through a synthesis can we begin
to set the broader trends of Scottish rural history in focus'.
Underlying his book is a belief that, in this period, 'the
relationship between land and society probably experienced
more continuity than discontinuity'. This evolutionary
perspective is served by eight chapters ranging from
prehistoric man and the Scottish landscape through the
central chapters on medieval Scotland, patterns of territorial
order in early Scottish society, the role and changing nature
of the medieval farming township 1100-1650, to two
regional reviews on rural economy and society in the south
and east 1650-1760 and in the Highlands and Islands
1650-1780.

As Dodgshon points out in Chapter 1, Scotland is rich in
prehistoric remains. The chief problem attached to their
value as sources is that many have still to be excavated, and
a further difficulty is that of those that have been
researched, relatively few have yielded clues on the exact
relationship between settlements, social groups, and
patterns of land use. Of course, this is not to say that we
know nothing of Scotland's early geographies for, as
Dodgshon illustrates using examples from south-west
Scotland, from Skara Brae and Rinyo and from several sites
in northern Scotland, there is much that can be observed
directly from the evidence (or inferred from the lack of it)
concerning the structure of prehistoric settlement,
continuity of location and the beginnings of shifting and
temporary cropping systems. But what the relative lack of
evidence for all Scotland in the prehistoric period means is
that we cannot firmly place or accurately date a *tabula rasa*
in early Scotland when, to one degree or another and allowing for some regional divergence, her occupants used the
land in established ways. The likelihood is that there never
was such a 'stage' in Scotland's transition from the
'prehistoric' to the 'early' to the 'medieval' period: separate
areas would have reflected the cultural and linguistic mix of
the time, and each district and people would have had
subtly different relationships between land use and popula-

tion. Continuity there may have been in settlement *location*
and even in the *type* of social relations in early Scotland, but
to use Dodgshon's own words, the 'gradual coalescing of
early peoples' would imply a period in Scotland's past when
discontinuity – of people, language, and patterns of
occupation – was more common than continuity. This is
not to deny Dodgshon's perspective of continuance and
evolution, merely to point to the difficulties of its measurement in the period before about 1100.

The evidence for patterns of territorial order in the
medieval period, particularly the multiple estate, is much
more certain. Dodgshon's third chapter is largely devoted to
an assessment of multiple estates from the point of view of
their physical make-up and distribution and their social
function. The likely diversity of the period leads him to
consider the 'real possibility that multiple estates were a
universal unit of territorial order in early Scotland, but cast
in a different terminological guise according to their
cultural or regional context'. This review of the admittedly
complex problem of 'shires' and 'thanages' is excellent:
wide-ranging in its coverage of the literature and in the
geography of the terms as understood and used in early
Scottish society and valuable also for the emphasis placed
upon the laying-over of new boundaries – on the land and
in society – that occurred with the expansion into Scotland
of the Anglo-Normans.

Feudalism and its analysis occupies a central place in the
book. Dodgshon seems a little uncertain how to regard the
term and how to assess its impact at the time. At one point
he writes that the topic cannot be seen as 'a discrete concept
that was introduced by David I . . . into a Scotland that was
innocent of its meaning' and then a few lines later notes that
'it would be quite wrong not to see the spread of Anglo-
Norman feudalism as marking an important point of
change', largely because feudalism offered the opportunity
'for transforming the pattern of landholding in Scotland'.
This initial uncertainty is not reflected in what follows:
admitting that 'Feudalism was not a static, unchanging
concept', Dodgshon assesses not only the varying regional
impact of change (and records, for example, how the
Highlands were last to feel the move towards feudalisation
and only did so in places), but also documents in some detail
what the shift to feudalism as the dominant mode of
production meant for those it affected and for the land they
worked. The exact reasons for the more general move
towards lease-holding, feuing, kindly tenure and tack-

holding are less clear, as is the relationship between population growth and economic change in the period 1100 to 1650. The basic social and economic unit of medieval Scotland was the farming township. It is in his analysis of the place of this unit in directing the above changes that Dodgshon's book has particular value. Increase in the number of settlements, the expansion of established settlements, and new processes of growth all mark the late medieval period as 'a vital one in the history of the Scottish rural society'. Just how vital the dimensions of change were depended on the time and place. Dodgshon argues for 'a burst of settlement formation' during the late fifteenth, sixteenth and seventeenth centuries. In his two regional chapters, he brings together the various strands of his argument in looking at farm sizes, their layout, the position of the tenantry, the different responses to a developing market economy and the legacy of past economies and social practices.

In his final chapter, Dodgshon writes that the transition from the 'Old' to the 'New' orders in the Highlands did not have 'the sharpness of chronology' that characterised the Lowlands: but even there, change was often varied in its impact. It is in illustrating these differences and in bringing together a range of diverse material upon rural economy, social practices and patterns of territorial order that his book succeeds so well. In its synthesis of information and in its interpretations of the assembled evidence, this is an important book.

Charles W J Withers

The Vernacular Architecture of Brittany,
Edinburgh 1982,   407 pp.   £30
G I Meirion-Jones

An enormous amount of information is packed into this double-column book, which encapsulates the results of a survey of the traditional buildings of Brittany, begun in 1970 and carried on with immense enthusiasm ever since. After setting the scene in terms of the physical and cultural landscape, which the author, as a historical geographer, does with considerable insight, Dr. Meirion-Jones goes on in logical sequence to examine the building materials and methods of construction. He then looks at a range of building forms, in part related to their scale − circular, sub-rectilinear, rectilinear, single-cell, longhouse, first-floor hall, two- and multi-cell. There follow chapters on farm buildings, and on hearth and home, and his Conclusion draws together the various threads.

Though some distance away from Scotland, there is nevertheless an astonishing range of parallels. Thatched houses with 'hangin' lums' (canopy chimneys), trusses that support the roof more or less independently of the side walls, clay buildings, roofs covered with clay and thatch, and many other constructional features of comparative interest are to

be found.

In some ways most valuable of all is the detailed discussion of the longhouse, a form of building where man and beast are housed in intercommunicating units under one roof. Though Jarlshof in Shetland includes ninth and tenth century longhouses (perhaps the earliest known in Britain), it is clearly impossible to say that the form is Scandinavian in origin when it is so widely distributed. Until the Agricultural Revolution led to a major rebuilding of houses in Lowland Scotland, up till about 1850, the longhouse was probably the main farm-house form to be found in Scotland. Longhouses have survived till the present day in the North and West of Scotland, including the evolved 'blackhouse' form, characterised by its double-skin walls. Elsewhere, the longhouse has been identified in Cumberland and Westmorland, Devon and Cornwall, Ireland and Wales. Now Meirion-Jones extends our knowledge of its range into Brittany in an admirably detailed way.

The whole book is clearly laid out with numerous plans, maps and illustrations, an extensive bibliography and a conjoint index and glossary.

A F

Deer Forests Landlords and Crofters, Edinburgh
1982,   226 pp.   £15
W Orr

This study of the Western Highlands in Victorian and Edwardian times is written by one who spent much of his life as a hill shepherd in the Western Highlands, before becoming an academic. Though writing as an academic, he does so with real insight born of practical experience. He writes without the sometimes misguided social motivation that often characterises social and economic historians with more urban backgrounds, and so succeeds in achieving a balanced appraisal of the interaction between landlord and tenant during the span 1850-1914. The driving forces were pressures of profitable industry in the south, to which the response of landlords, whether of native stock or increasingly from outside, was limited by the limited number of options available in the area under study.

In dealing with the laws and development of deer forests, Orr effectively fills the historical gap that follows the decline of hill sheep farming after the period of the so-called Clearances. The book, therefore, is a substantial contribution to the history of Highland sheep farming; and as a practical man, Orr also examines alternatives to deer forests, particularly through the formation of club farms, the incidence of which was surprisingly wide, but whose fortunes tended to hang on the slender thread of reasonable weather.

He also examines the economics of deer forests in relation to the estates, and to the contribution made by them directly or indirectly through rates, employment, etc. to the economics of their areas; the social impact on the crofters, through eviction, re-employment, loss of an effective middle class, and even as reflected in open conflict which could result from a certain degree of political stimulation from the Highland Land League. Government efforts to resolve seemingly insoluble problems are also glanced at.

The text is eminently readable. The Appendices act as a handbook covering sheep and wool prices, wintering costs, ratios of sheep and cattle numbers, the chronology of deer forest development, their valuations, a full listing of deer forests, estate rents and expenditure, numbers employed on forests, and beef and cattle prices over the relevant period.

A F

Traditional Farm Buildings in North-East Wales 1550-1900, Welsh Folk Museum 1982, 333 pp.
E Wiliam

This new book follows two pioneer works on Welsh houses which had much influence in Wales and beyond. These are Dr. I. C. Peate's *The Welsh House* (1940), and the three volumes of *Monmouthshire Houses* by Sir Cyril Fox and Lord Raglan. The present study is more limited in scope, and concentrates entirely on farm buildings, recorded through systematic field surveying in 1974-79 in North-East Wales, now the county of Clwyd.

Using his skills as a trained archaeologist, Eurwyn Wiliam examines in close detail a ten per cent example of farmsteads built before 1900. Numerous distribution maps and statistical tables are used, and these, with survey plans, are related to the background history, geography and geology of the region.

The various chapters cover siting and layout, building materials and the financing, design and development of farm-buildings. The major steading units – barn, stable, byre, dairy, cartshed, granary – are examined, as well as smaller units – pigsty, brewhouse, gorse-mill, poultry house, dovecote. The methodology of approach is outlined, and there is a useful bibliography.

This is an important work, which gives a new scientific dimension to the study of farm-buildings.

A F

Från vildmark till bygd. En etnologisk undersökning av nybyggkulturen i Lappland före industrialismens genombrott (Norrländska Skrifter Nr. 10), Umeå 1982
Å Campbell

It is a pleasure to welcome a facsimile re-issue of this important, pioneering book, which first appeared in 1948. It is a study of the processes of change in Lapland 'from

wilderness to settled country' during the eighteenth and nineteenth centuries. Sub-titled 'an ethnological investigation of the culture of colonists in Lapland before the impact of industrialisation', it shows how a sub-arctic wilderness was tamed and how the Swedes and indigenous nomads interacted.

The story runs from medieval times, when the pelt and fur trade made the Swedish Crown look with profit-making eyes at this northern land's resources. Taxation was enforced, and since it had to be provided in kind, the fauna was decimated. A compensatory development of fishing and reindeer-breeding took place, changing the older way of life of the Lapps.

This led to some rivalry between the Lapps and Swedish farmers who periodically visited the country for fishing. Missionaries who settled there to christianise the natives, became the first farmers. The mining of iron ore also began. There followed a period of colonising activity, by Swedes, Finns and Lapps, aided by advantage-giving Swedish ordinances of 1673, 1695 and 1749. The round of work was controlled by the environment. Some concentrated on fishing, hunting and trapping, and others based their existence on cattle-breeding. Cropping came later as settlers worked out where frost-free grounds lay.

Contact between peoples was also coloured by the sub-arctic conditions. Where these are extreme, mutual aid becomes a necessity, at least for a time. Causes of contention lay in the way resources were shared or exploited. There would be rivalry in fishing and to some extent hunting and trapping; reindeer pasture was destroyed by cattle and horses; colonisers' dogs frightened reindeer; reindeer destroyed hay-stacks and drying hurdles; burning as a means of clearing ground for cropping affected both forest and pasture. The Swedes left the Lapps to herd the reindeer, which had to graze over the colonists' land, and made of them dependent herdsmen. They also introduced the custom of brandy drinking, which led to excesses, till checked by the Læstadian Revival and the introduction of coffee.

Such a rough outline scarcely does justice to a book that contains many lessons for the nature of the spread of settlement, and the introduction of different values.

This issue contains a biography, by Dr Åsa Nyman, of Professor Åke Campbell (1891-1957), who played a basic part in the development of ethnology as an academic subject in Sweden. He was well-known in Ireland and in Scotland, making a special study of the Hebrides where he tested the meeting of Celtic and Nordic forms of culture, using building-, cultivation-, and cattle husbandry techniques as his keystones, no doubt keeping in mind the methods of investigation he had developed for Lapland.

These methods are discussed in a second contribution to the volume, by Professor Phebe Fjellström. She points out that acculturation and ecology played dominant roles in

Campbell's thinking, and he saw his work in Lapland as having international perspectives in these respects.

For theoretical and practical purposes, a translation into English would be both welcome and useful.

A F

Ethnologia Europaea, 'A World Review of European Ethnology', deals with both theoretical and practical aspects of ethnology in the European sense. The *1981 (XII, 2)* issue contains articles on questions relating, for example, to the European joint family, neighbourhood groups in Rumania and West Germany, and the place of scents and aromatic plants in rituals relating to the main milestones in human life and the protection of stock and the home.

Of special interest is Gösta Berg's contribution on the Swedish Threshing Wagon, a device that knocked out ears of grain by being drawn over the sheaves. It took the form of sets of heavy wheels with cross-bars, or of wooden rollers fitted with spikes or flanges. Its particular significance is that it marks a stage, aimed at speeding up the threshing process, that lies midway between the use of hand-operated flails and the adoption of threshing-mills. It does not appear to have been used in Britain, though the spread of the roller in other countries seems to be due to the influence of Sweden.

This issue includes an obituary notice of Professor Kustaa Vilkuna, 1902-1980, for long a leading figure in Finnish and in European ethnology. As farmer, lexicographer, ethnologist and politician, he led a full and valuable life, publishing well over 1,000 articles and books in his lifetime. A personal comment may be added − I knew him as a friend from the time of my first international conference in Sweden, in the early 1960s. There, in the course of an evening's talk, he held out his large, firm hand, shook mine, and said 'Jag hedder Kustaa' (my name is Kustaa) − a friendly establishment of first-name terms that typified his humanity.

The *1982/83 (XIII, 1)* issue also contains much of interest. It lays emphasis on the popular culture of the Romance countries, particularly Spain, France, Italy and Sicily.

Claude Rival offers an interesting study of tidal mills in France. There seems to have been one dated between 1067 and 1082 at the entrance to Dover Harbour, but French records go back only to the twelfth century. Almost a hundred examples have been noted in France, Germany, Holland, Belgium. North-west Spain and Portugal also had them. They were exported to the eastern coast of America in the early seventeenth century, and were still being built in France in the nineteenth century. It should be noted that Scotland had them as well, for example at Petty in Inverness (abandoned 1825) and at Munlochy in Cromarty.

From Poland comes an article by Z. Kłodnicki, E. Kłosek and A. Szymański on the classification of European types of flails. There is a rich literature on this subject, and the authors look at it critically in order to bring it up-to-date. In terms of typology, 30 flail-types are distinguished, tabularised and illustrated by diagrams.

Ethnologia Europaea appears annually, extending to about 240 pages. It is available from the Verlag Otto Schwartz and Co., D-3400 Göttingen, Annastrasse 7, Germany, at a cost of *c.* 48 German marks. The journal's wide coverage, geographical and methodological, gives it a special degree of importance in the growth of European ethnology as an academic subject.

A F

LOADS AND ROADS
IN SCOTLAND AND BEYOND
Edited by Alexander Fenton and Geoffrey Stell
0 85976 107 X   160 pages 62 illus. £8.50

The aim of this book is to give historians, geographers, engineers, archaeologists and students of place-names and material culture a lively and realistic picture of the ways in which our ancestors overcame difficulties of transport and communications and to show the links between prehistory, the Roman and medieval periods, and the more recent past.

Contents: *J. M. Coles:* Prehistoric Roads and Trackways in Britain — Problems and Possibilities. *G. S. Maxwell:* The Evidence from the Roman Period. *G. W. S. Barrow:* Land Routes — the Medieval Evidence. *E. Ruddock:* Bridges and Roads in Scotland, 1400-1750. *G. Hay & G. Stell:* Old Bridge, Bridge of Earn — a Posthumous Account. *A. Fenton:* Wheelless Transport in Northern Scotland. *A. Fenton:* The Distribution of Carts and Wagons. Index.

SCOTTISH COUNTRY LIFE
Alexander Fenton
0 85976 011 1   266 pages 120 illus. £7.00

'This must be the definitive work on the subject. The vast and varied field of agricultural practice during the centuries and over all Scotland is his subject, and he writes engagingly with unobtrusive scholarship of its every aspect — farming practice, implements, drains, dykes, crafts, fairs and markets, food and drink. At a time when mechanisation and standardisation is the rule, this book is more than ever valuable, and must become a standard source for future generations to study and enjoy.' *National Trust Newsletter*

'This book is a veritable treasurehouse of factual material appertaining to country life as it has been lived through the centuries, not only in the Scottish Lowlands but also in the Highlands and Islands.' *Scots Magazine*

'This is a fascinating and important book.' *Scotsman*

THE SCOTTISH ANTIQUARIAN TRADITION
Essays to mark the Bicentenary of the Society
of Antiquaries of Scotland
A. S. Bell
0 85976 080 4   296 pages 10 illus. £15.00

'A sparkling collection of essays, reflecting light on more than the obscurer recesses of the Society of Antiquaries of Scotland. It throws light on the early development of archaeology in Great Britain and it shows that while much may change, people and the problems they cause don't. This book should be on every archaeologist's, historian's and sociologist's bookshelf.' *Popular Archaeology*

John Donald Publishers Ltd, 138 St Stephen Street, Edinburgh, Scotland.

THE NORTHERN ISLES

Alexander Fenton

0 85976 019 7   732 pages 287 illus. £18.00

'It is a delight and a privilege to welcome a new book by Alexander Fenton which recreates the physical environment in which the people lived, the work with crops and beasts, the harvest of the sea, the houses, the food they ate. It is a massive piece of scholarship, an encyclopaedia of the material culture of Orkney and Shetland, and will assuredly become the classic work of reference in this field for many years to come. An indispensable work for anyone interested in the traditional life of Orkney and Shetland.' *New Shetlander*

THE RURAL ARCHITECTURE OF SCOTLAND

Alexander Fenton and Bruce Walker

0 85976 020 0   256 pages 195 illus. £15.00

'*The Rural Architecture of Scotland* has achieved a multi-disciplinary approach to its subject through the contrasting expertise of its two authors. This combination of skills is of especial importance in the study of farm architecture where a knowledge of the form of agricultural buildings is meaningless without an appreciation of their function.

'The quality and scope of the illustrations is very high. They include sketches, plans and photographs from recent field surveys, engravings from early printed works and the oustanding archive photographs from collections like the George Washington Wilson.

'The publishers, who are beginning to accumulate a formidable list of books on Scottish social and economic history, deserve praise for the clear and legible format of *The Rural Architecture of Scotland*. As an introduction to the present state of knowledge it succeeds admirably in its purpose. Future architectural and agricultural historians of Scotland will need to draw extensively upon this work.' *Museums Journal*

THE NORTHERN AND WESTERN ISLES
IN THE VIKING WORLD

Alexander Fenton and Hermann Pálsson

0 85976 101 0   300 pages 60 illus. £20.00

This book, which celebrates the bicentenary of the National Museum of Antiquities of Scotland, brings together information from the fields of archaeology, ethnology, language, literature, history and oral tradition to show how these together can be used to interpret different periods in the past. Much of the material is new and original and reflects the range of research which the Museum covers.

John Donald Publishers Ltd, 138 St Stephens Street, Edinburgh, Scotland

FOOD IN PERSPECTIVE
Third International Conference of Ethnological Food Research
Alexander Fenton and Trefor M. Owen
0 85976 044 8   440 pages 60 illus. £20.00

'This is a well-produced and well-balanced collection of essays and will be welcomed in an English-speaking world which, some thirty years ago, was well served by historians of food, but has in recent years seen almost all the valuable research on the subject being done in France.' *Museums Journal*

'As every country is bound up with food production and trade, this study is a most valuable contribution to the knowledge of all nations.' *Lore and Language*

Contents: The World Food Crisis, Ethnological Food Research, and Museums. A Preference Food: The Philadelphia Soft Pretzel. The Thrive-Bit — A Study of Cultural Adaptation. Bread in Ireland. Some Symbolic Aspects of Food Products in the Light of a Thirteenth Century Polish Historical Source. The Social Functions of Festival Food: A Few Thoughts on an Investigation in Northern Sweden. The Privileged Position of Farinaceous Foods in Austria. The Cookery Book as a Document for Cultural and Social History. Frozen Dinners — the Staple Emergency: Meals of a Changing Modern Society. Food and Meals in a Congested District: County Donegal in 1891. The Significance of Food in Religious Ideology and Behaviour in Marathi Myths. Plants and Weeds as Food of the People: An Example from West Steiermark, Austria. Freshly Consumed Flat Bread in the near East. Ethnological Characteristics of Traditional Wheat Flour Foods in Bulgaria. The Diffusion Channels of Urban Food Habits. Starting an Anthropology Handbook on Food Habits for the Knowledge of Man's Food Behaviour. The Diet of Women in Childbirth. The Preference for Sweets, Spices and Almond Milk in Late Medieval English Cuisine. The Making of Health Wine in the Fifteenth Century in Hungary, and the Role of Wine in the Diet and Medicine of the People at the Present Day. The Social Aspects of the Diet of the Polish People, with Special Reference to Preferences and Taboos. The Potato in Finnish Food Economy. The Beginnings of the Modern Milk Age in Germany. Greek Immigrant Cuisine in America: Continuity and Change. On the Origins and Development of Preferences and Taboos in Eating and Drinking. The Impact of the Introduction of Maize into the Food of the Rumanian People. The First Ethnic Cook Book in the United States. An Interdependence of Foodways and Architecture: A Foodways Context on the American Plains. Food and Traditional Verbal Modes in the Social Control of Children. Food in a Medical System: Prescriptions and Proscriptions in Health and Illness among Malays. The Use of Cannabis in two Cookery Books of the Fifteenth Century. The Sausage Culture of the Pennsylvania Germans.

John Donald Publishers Ltd, 138 St Stephen Street, Edinburgh, Scotland

ROSC

The aim of the *Review of Scottish Culture* is to fill a gap that exists in the study of Scottish Material culture. Scotland has a long history covering ten thousand years and in the course of that time it has been greatly affected by the cultures of neighbouring peoples, some of them invaders. Scottish influence on the world at large, spread by the wandering Scot, is proverbial and *The Review of Scottish Culture* will in its varied contributions, throw fresh light on these inward and outward movements, where necessary tracing them beyond the bounds of Scotland itself.

Review of Scottish Culture will concentrate on the material aspects of the country's social and economic history, the ethnology of Scotland, and will cover rural and urban, maritime and land based topics alike, the applied and decorative arts, graphics and design, and the actions and interactions of the people of the country.

The contributions will deal with original source material in a readable form so that the readership will not be confined to the specialist but will include all those interested in the culture of Scotland.

The acronym ROSC is appropriate, since its meaning in Gaelic relates to the action of seeing — vision, perception, understanding — and also to what is seen — the written word in prose. The essence of this philosophical sense will be reflected in the contents of *Review of Scottish Culture.*

The volumes in this series will undoubtedly become an important source of information on the ethnology of Scotland and if you wish to ensure that you receive all volumes as they are published please complete the order form and send it to **John Donald Publishers Ltd, 138 St Stephen Street, Edinburgh EH3 5AA** and all volumes will be sent to you as they become available.

Order Form
Please send and charge to me each volume of *Review of Scottish Culture* as published.

Name..

Address ....

....

....